水面波纹

[美国]盖瑞·施耐德 著
西川 译

译林出版社

图书在版编目（CIP）数据

水面波纹：汉英对照／（美）盖瑞·施耐德（Gary Snyder）著；西川译．—南京：译林出版社，2017.10

（镜中丛书）

书名原文：Ripples on the Surface

ISBN 978-7-5447-6917-4

Ⅰ.①水… Ⅱ.①盖… ②西… Ⅲ.①诗集－美国－现代－汉、英 Ⅳ.①I712.25

中国版本图书馆 CIP 数据核字（2017）第 086680 号

著作权合同登记号　图字：10-2013-243号

水面波纹［美国］盖瑞·施耐德／著　西川／译

责任编辑　吴莹莹
装帧设计　韦　枫
责任印制　颜　亮

出版发行　译林出版社
地　　址　南京市湖南路 1 号 A 楼
邮　　箱　yilin@yilin.com
网　　址　www.yilin.com
市场热线　025-86633278
排　　版　南京展望文化发展有限公司
印　　刷　恒美印务（广州）有限公司
开　　本　889 毫米 ×1010 毫米　1/32
印　　张　7.125
插　　页　4
版　　次　2017 年 10 月第 1 版　2017 年 10 月第 1 次印刷
书　　号　ISBN 978-7-5447-6917-4
定　　价　58.00 元

“镜中丛书”总序

自2010年起，由我主持的“国际诗人在香港”项目，每年邀请一两位著名的国际诗人，分别与优秀的译者合作，除了举办诗歌工作坊、朗诵会等一系列诗歌活动，更重要的是，由香港牛津大学出版社出版双语对照诗集的丛书。到目前为止，已有八位应邀的国际诗人和译者合作出版了八本诗集，形成了一个小小的传统。这套丛书再从香港到内地，从繁体版到简体版，由译林出版社出版，取名为“镜中丛书”。按原出版时间顺序，包括谷川俊太郎、迈克·帕尔玛、德拉戈莫申科、盖瑞·施耐德、阿多尼斯和特朗斯特罗默的六本诗集。

与此并行的是“香港国际诗歌之夜”——自2009年起创办的香港国际诗歌节，每两年一届。这两个诗歌项目交织互补，为香港提供独特的文化平台，进一步形成汉语诗歌与国际诗歌的双重推动力。

这套丛书的设想基于以下考虑：首先，在国际诗人与汉语译者的文本互动之中，跨越语言的边界；其二，对多语种的译者提出挑战，为丰富现代汉语提供新的品质及方向；其三，在国际诗人、译者和读者之间，在文本对应与参照中，构成某种内在张力，激活一连串语言内外的连锁反应。

这套丛书首先面对的是院校外语专业的大学生，以及初学或精通外语的读者，当然也包括学者、译者和诗人同行。

“镜中丛书”是我和同行合作编辑出版的中英、中法等一系列双语对照诗集丛书的“兄弟姐妹”，共同组成了一个国际诗歌的“大家庭”。诗歌是人类精神家园的保证，也是一个民族苦难中的幸运。

北岛

2015 年 7 月 21 日

盖瑞·施耐德（廖伟棠摄于香港维多利亚港）

目录

选自《观浪》

选自《龟岛》

选自《斧子把》

选自《无性》

集外

译者前言

本书收有一首名为《柿子》的诗，作于1984年，而且在诗末盖瑞·施耐德还特别注明，该诗写于北京。那一年，“文革”以后的第一个美国作家代表团来华访问，参加第二届中美作家会议（第一届1982年在美国举办），动静颇大。代表团成员除了盖瑞·施耐德，还有艾伦·金斯堡、库尔特·冯内古特、托尼·莫里森、汤婷婷、哈里森·索尔兹伯里等。我当时尚在北大英文系读书。施耐德和金斯堡来北大朗诵。既然当时我已被称作“校园诗人”了，他们的朗诵我肯定是不能漏掉的。记得他们的朗诵地点是在一间大教室里。那大概是我第一次见到文学界世界级的大人物。教室里挤满了听众。我找不到地方，只好跑到第一排座位的前面，坐到地上，我和朗诵者只相距不到两米远。金斯堡坐在椅子上用他的自制手风琴伴奏，朗诵了一些他自己的诗，但我记得最清楚的是他唱诵英国诗人威廉·布莱克的《老虎》。他边唱边操控手风琴，同时双脚在木制讲台上跺出节拍。后来他们又去了外国语学院（现在的北京外国语大学）朗诵。我也去了，可见我成了他们的铁杆粉丝。朗诵会地点是一座礼堂。我记得轮到施耐德朗诵，他要求大家都站起来，并且还要求大家都举起右手。我已记不清他当时朗诵了什么，但他朗诵时全场的气氛令我至今记忆犹新。那像是一个仪式，很庄严。此前我还从未见识过那样的朗诵。那次经历令我对从书本上读来的“垮掉派”有了切身体验。中国书本上的“垮掉派”，既是反抗的，也是颓废堕落的，但1984年，我看到了“垮掉派”严肃的理想主义的一面。没想到时隔二十八年，我成了盖瑞·施耐德的中文译者。

施耐德、金斯堡、凯鲁亚克这些人，从某种意义上说，改变了二战以后世界文化的氛围。他们对当时美国社会的道德状况、文化状况、政治秩序的批判和反抗，他们身体力行的新的生活方式，曾经令那时的美国青年，乃至整个保守的西方发抖。他们这样的精神诉求和生活方式在“文革”以后迅速传入中国，引起了当时中国大城市里——如北京、上海等地——年轻一代的共鸣。大家先是通过一些外国文学杂志、外国当代诗选阅读他们作品的译文。1985年上海外语教育出版社出版的莫里斯·迪克斯坦因著《伊甸园之门——六十年代美国文化》(方晓光译)一书，更让人们了解到垮掉派文学、嬉皮士运动的真貌。后来凯鲁亚克的《在路上》中译本(1990)、金斯堡的诗选中译本(2000)等也得以陆续在大陆出版。直到今天，更年轻的人们在读到他们的作品时，依然会有一种受到鼓舞的感觉。中国青年所面对的当然是中国的社会、道德、文化现实，但大家从垮掉派文学中认识到反抗和批判对于一种文化的重要性，认识到“另一种生活”并非不能来到我们身旁。所以，2011年8月，当北岛从香港打电话给我，问我能否翻译盖瑞·施耐德的诗歌时，我立刻就答应了。

施耐德在中国的诗歌读者中虽然大名鼎鼎，但遗憾的是，出于种种原因，大陆始终没有出版过他诗歌和散文的单行本。台湾联合文学出版社在1979年出版过一本由林耀福、梁秉钧编选的施耐德诗文选《山即是心》(多人译)。我们在网络上能够搜到的施耐德诗歌的中译文中有不少来自这本书。台湾的《当代》杂志曾在1990年9月第53期上刊出《诗人史耐德：从敲打派到后现代》的专辑。据说香港浸会大学的钟玲教授在台湾出版过一本研究性著作《美国诗人史耐德与亚洲文化》，惜不曾见到。大陆这边由于不曾出版过能够较全面反映施耐德面貌的书，因而读者对施耐德的印象往往极为简单：他是垮掉派（台湾译作“敲打派”）中的重要诗人；他受到过中国古代文化的重要影响；他翻译了《寒山诗》并影响巨大。除此之外我们对施耐德所知甚少。例如，即使在他与中国古代文学、文化的关系方面，我们绝大多数人也不了解：他还是白居易《长恨歌》的英译者，他还热爱陆游，还翻译过孟浩然、王维、王之涣、王昌龄、杜甫、杜牧、元稹、刘长卿、柳宗元等人的诗。施耐德最重要的长诗之一《溪山无尽》为他在1997年赢得素负盛名的波林根诗歌奖。这部长诗的名字来自现藏美国克利夫兰美术馆的宋或金佚名画家所绘《溪山无尽图》。我见到过有人在文章中提及施耐德的这部长诗，但诗题胡乱译为什么《山河无尽》、《山水无边》之类，显然是译者不知道有这么一件中国绘画杰作的存在。如果单就我们能够找到的施耐德诗歌的中译文看，我发现也存在许多问题：首先，出现在中文里的施耐德诗歌多为他的早期作品；其次，不同的译者大多挑选他容易翻译的诗歌来翻；第三，也是最重要的，许多中译文谬误百出。

这造成了施耐德诗歌在中文环境里的传播之误。除了误译，中文读者，尤其是大陆读者，对施耐德的写作背景、精神背景显然缺乏完整的了解。仅从本书所选施耐德的短诗看，我们就会发现他与日本文化、佛教禅宗（尤其是日本禅宗）的密切关系。1956 年施耐德获美国第一禅宗学院奖修金东渡日本，在京都修习禅宗、日文、中文和梵文，一住就是十二年。他娶了日本太太，翻译过日本诗人宫泽贤治的诗，与诗人七尾榊结下了深厚的友谊，并且在某种程度上受到了七尾榊的影响。施耐德与东方的关系还不仅限于对中国和日本的阅读、体验与观察。在日本期间，他曾有六个月的时间与艾伦·金斯堡、琼妮·基格在印度、尼泊尔旅行，参禅礼佛，走访胜迹。他本人还到过斯里兰卡、印度尼西亚等地，甚至曾随一艘油轮到过土耳其伊斯坦布尔。这一切经验都反映在了他的写作和思考之中。但是，说到底，施耐德是一位太平洋一侧的美国诗人。他生于旧金山。两岁前与家人移居西雅图。后来又与母亲和妹妹迁居俄勒冈州的波特兰。1969 年他自日本返回美国后，一直生活在内华达山脉北部的玉巴河畔。他自小对北美印第安人文化，尤其是印第安人对大自然的态度深感兴趣。为施耐德在 1975 年赢得普利策奖的诗集《龟岛》（纽约新方向出版社出版），书名便取自印第安人称呼大地的古语。这里透露出诗人受到印第安文化影响的对自然环境的深切关注。1992 年纽约万神殿出版社出版了他的《无性：新诗及诗选》，该书获得美国国家图书奖提名。在为这本书所写的序言中，施耐德说："这些诗歌属于（美国）西海岸语言风格，属于盎格鲁-法兰克美国的印欧文化，以及迅然呈现的太平洋文化。这里有些诗受益于我对中国和日本短诗的阅读，有些诗受益于少数族裔诗歌的写法，而最使我受益的是 20 世纪中叶的那些大家巨子。我还要向美国的土著歌曲、故事以及生计本身鞠躬致谢，我还要向其鞠躬的是边远西部丰茂的森林、冰峰雪岭和一些伟大的教师。"

盖瑞·施耐德的生平，读者从附录在本书后面的"年表"就可了解，兹不赘述。但是关于他的生平、写作和成就，有一点需要我们格外关注，那就是，施耐德不仅仅是一位诗人，或者说，他是一位极其特殊的诗人。在整个垮掉派诗人、作家、艺术家群体里，施耐德的精神背景和生活经历都非常特殊。以至于有美国论者认为，严格说来，施耐德虽属于"旧金山文艺复兴"，但自他远赴日本，他就与其他垮掉派成员在写作和生活方式上拉开了距离（当然情感上他始终认同垮掉派群体）。施耐德是一个行动的人，重实践的人，对自己的理想身体力行。早在少年时代他就成了一名登山好手。后来在波特兰的瑞德学院和加州大学伯克利分校读书期间，他将一部分时间用于当伐木工、筑路工、森林火情瞭望员、海员等等。体力劳动和佛教冥想使他对生活、社会、大自然有了深入的体验，并与大自然建立起一份特殊的关系。他因此成了土地、树木、野兽、鱼类和飞鸟的代言人。他可能是这个世界上较早觉悟到人类应该善待大自然、保护大自然的先行者之一。他倡导一种大地意识，并从这种意识出发，对种种美国和世界的社会问题、生态问题、政治问题展开思考和批判。于是我们在施耐德身上既看到了诗人，又看到了行动者，也看到了标准的美国左派知识分子。这一切因素又反过头来作用于施耐德的写作。按照美国批评家查尔斯·阿尔铁里在《庙堂扩建：六十年代美国诗歌新方向》一书中表达的观点，施耐德既创造了一种独立于西方文化的宗教信仰，也创造了一种新型诗歌，这种诗歌直接、具体、非浪漫，具有生物学特征。这使得他获得了一种新的视角，可以强有力地处理形而上学。施耐德的写作展开在对自然、宗教、文化、社会、历史、思想等多方面问题的关注上，他所取得的成就，据一些论者，可能是垮掉一代诗人中最高的。

如前所述，盖瑞·施耐德不仅是一位诗人。他在散文写作和文学翻译等方面同样取得了很高的成就。他的散文作品《大地家族》已经成为美国当代文学的经典之作。但本书不是施耐德读本或选集，而仅仅是一本施耐德的诗选，而且是一本短诗选。不过即使这样，我依然希望本诗选能够在一定程度上展现一个多方面的施耐德。收入本书的大多数诗篇都是由施耐德本人从他的诗选集《无性》中挑选的，最后一首《夜晚故事》是他的新作。这与台湾那本《山即是心》所选篇目重合的部分很少，所以两本书似乎有一种互补的关系。施耐德的诗歌相当难译，他使用的词语，有些来自北太平洋美国人的小区语言，有些来自印第安部落语言，词典上根本找不到。有些词语即使词典上有，施耐德也不是在一般意义上使用；即使他在一般意义上使用，他也可能赋予了它们多重含义。书中所收不少诗篇的写作背景与日本有关，查找和搜索按日语发音拼写的日本人名、地名、专有名词的汉字写法成了一件巨大的苦差事。其个别诗歌以前被翻译成中文时，译者索性省略了日语词语的汉字书写，或者在中译文中干脆保留了字母拼写，这在我看来至少是偷懒和不严肃的。本书力求在这一方面做到完善。书中个别涉日名字、名词我请教了久居日本的诗人、翻译家田原。施耐德诗歌还涉及印度文化、印第安文化，以及一些类似伐木、烧窑、机械、航海、天文等方面的专业术语和知识，我也尽量使译文能够追上原文。进行这样复杂的翻译仅靠我一个人根本无法完成。在翻译的过程中，我得到了几位美国朋友的关键的帮助，他们是 Lucas Klein、Christopher Lupke、Christopher Arigo，他们纠正了我的一些误译之处，对原文中一些我不理解的地方给予了解答。此外，我还应提及美国著名的中国古代诗歌译者比尔·波特（笔名 Red Pine）。比尔·波特送给了我许多与盖瑞·施耐德有关的图书数据。我在此由衷地感谢他们。我最要感谢的当然是盖瑞·施耐德本人。他是一个工作非常认真仔细的人。在我刚开始动手翻译他的作品时，他就寄来了他从前对其西班牙语、日语译者所提问题的解答，这对我帮助不小。最后约有十几个问题，我依然无法解决，只好请教施耐德本人，得到了他耐心的解释。当然我还要感谢诗人北岛，如果不是他的建议甚至催促，可能就没有这本书。也许书中依然存在一些缺点，敬希读者指正。

西川

2012 年 2 月 20 日

水面波纹

盖瑞· 施耐德诗选

Mid-August at Sourdough Mountain Lookout

Down valley a smoke haze
Three days heat, after five days rain
Pitch glows on the fir-cones
Across rocks and meadows
Swarms of new flies.

I cannot remember things I once read
A few friends, but they are in cities.
Drinking cold snow-water from a tin cup
Looking down for miles
Through high still air.

八月中旬在苏窦山瞭望站

山谷下一阵烟岚
三天暑热，之前五日大雨
冷杉球果上树脂闪耀
新生的苍蝇
团团飞过岩石和草地。

我想不起曾经读过的东西
有几个朋友，但住在城里。
喝锡罐中冷冷的雪水
向下远眺，数英里在目
大气高旷而静止。

Piute Creek

One granite ridge
A tree, would be enough
Or even a rock, a small creek,
A bark shred in a pool.
Hill beyond hill, folded and twisted
Tough trees crammed
In thin stone fractures
A huge moon on it all, is too much.
The mind wanders. A million
Summers, night air still and the rocks
Warm. Sky over endless mountains.
All the junk that goes with being human
Drops away, hard rock wavers
Even the heavy present seems to fail
This bubble of a heart.
Words and books
Like a small creek off a high ledge
Gone in the dry air.

A clear, attentive mind

皮尤特涧

一条花岗岩山脊
一棵树，即已足够
甚至只要一块岩石、一道溪流、
池塘里的一块树皮，即可。
群山层峦叠嶂
树木粗壮，挤在
石罅之间；
月照万有，太大的月亮。
思绪漫漫，一百万个
夏日，夜气静而山岩暖。
长空笼盖无尽的群山。
人类带来的一切废物
尽去，盘石颤抖
即使沉重的现在似乎也无法应对
这气泡的心。
词语和书籍
像泻下高崖的小溪
消失在干燥的空气中。

一个了无心思的心灵

Has no meaning but that

Which sees is truly seen.

No one loves rock, yet we are here.

Night chills. A flick

In the moonlight

Slips into Juniper shadow:

Back there unseen

Cold proud eyes

Of Cougar or Coyote

Watch me rise and go.

清澈，敏感
看到的就是真正看见的。
无人爱岩石，而我们在这里。
夜凉。月色中
一个闪光
闪入落叶松的阴影：
那里，隐蔽之处
狮子或土狼的眼睛
冷傲地
注视我起身，离开。

Milton by Firelight

Piute Creek, August 1955

"O hell, what do mine eyes
    with grief behold?"
Working with an old
Singlejack miner, who can sense
The vein and cleavage
In the very guts of rock, can
Blast granite, build
Switchbacks that last for years
Under the beat of snow, thaw, mule-hooves.
What use, Milton, a silly story
Of our lost general parents,
    eaters of fruit?

The Indian, the chainsaw boy,
And a string of six mules
Came riding down to camp
Hungry for tomatoes and green apples.

火畔读弥尔顿

皮尤特涧，1955 年 8 月

“哦地狱，我这悲伤的眼睛
　　看见了什么？”
与一位使锤的老矿工
一起干活，他能觉察
矿脉的走向和岩石内脏的
绺裂，他能
炸开花岗岩，开出
盘曲的道路，令它能历经
雪冻冰融、骡蹄践踏的节律
而固持多年。
弥尔顿，你的蠢故事何用之有，
讲我们湮没的始祖
　　那吃野果的人？

那使链锯的印第安男孩
赶着一溜六头骡子
来到营地
饥饿地寻找西红柿和绿苹果。

Sleeping in saddle-blankets

Under a bright night-sky

Han River slantwise by morning.

Jays squall

Coffee boils

In ten thousand years the Sierras

Will be dry and dead, home of the scorpion.

Ice-scratched slabs and bent trees.

No paradise, no fall,

Only the weathering land

The wheeling sky,

Man, with his Satan

Scouring the chaos of the mind.

Oh Hell!

Fire down

Too dark to read, miles from a road

The bell-mare clangs in the meadow

That packed dirt for a fill-in

Scrambling through loose rocks

On an old trail

All of a summer's day.

在明亮的夜空下
他睡去，盖着亦当马鞍用的毛毯
黎明时分，河汉倾斜。
樫鸟啼鸣
咖啡煮开

万年以后这内华达群山
将干燥死寂，成为蝎子的家园。
有冰刻的石板和弯曲的树木。
没有乐园，没有堕落，
只有日晒风吹的土地
旋转的天空，
人类，和他的撒旦
将洗刷心灵的混乱。
哦，地狱！

火熄了
太暗，没法读了，道路一侧数里之遥
草地上的母马脖铃叮当
一整个夏季的一天
泥土厚积，填塞坑洼
一条经年小道
蜿蜒在乱石之间。

Above Pate Valley

We finished clearing the last
Section of trail by noon,
High on the ridge-side
Two thousand feet above the creek
Reached the pass, went on
Beyond the white pine groves,
Granite shoulders, to a small
Green meadow watered by the snow,
Edged with Aspen—sun
Straight high and blazing
But the air was cool.
Ate a cold fried trout in the
Trembling shadows. I spied
A glitter, and found a flake
Black volcanic glass—obsidian—
By a flower. Hands and knees
Pushing the Bear grass, thousands
Of arrowhead leavings over a
Hundred yards. Not one good

佩特谷上方

中午时分我们清理完
最后一段小路，
这里高居于山脊边缘
下距溪涧两千英尺
到达隘口之后再往前
高于白色的松林
花岗岩肩头，就到达一小片
被雪水浇灌的绿色草地
周围有白杨环绕——阳光
当头直射
但空气清凉。
在颤抖的阴影里
吃一条冷了的烤鳟鱼。
在一朵花旁，我瞥见
闪光，发现一片
黑色的火山熔岩玻璃——
黑曜石。手脚并用
拨开丝兰草，但见百码之内
遗存着数千枚箭镞。
没有一枚完好，全是

Head, just razor flakes
On a hill snowed all but summer,
A land of fat summer deer,
They came to camp. On their
Own trails. I followed my own
Trail here. Picked up the cold-drill,
Pick, singlejack, and sack
Of dynamite.
Ten thousand years.

锋利的小石片，在这座

除了夏天三季落雪的山上

夏天，肥硕的鹿

到此扎营。它们有

自己的路径。在这儿

我也走自己的小道

拾起钢钎

鹤嘴锄、大铁锤，和

炸药包。

一万年。

Thin Ice

Walking in February
A warm day after a long freeze
On an old logging road
Below Sumas Mountain
Cut a walking stick of alder,
Looked down through clouds
On wet fields of the Nooksack—
And stepped on the ice
Of a frozen pool across the road.
It creaked
The white air under
Sprang away, long cracks
Shot out in the black,
My cleated mountain boots
Slipped on the hard slick
—like thin ice—the sudden
Feel of an old phrase made real—
Instant of frozen leaf,
Icewater, and staff in hand.
"Like walking on thin ice— "

薄冰

二月，漫长的寒冷过后
一个暖和的日子
走在苏马斯山下
一条陈年的伐木之路上
砍下一根桤木拐杖，
透过云层俯览
努克塞克湿漉漉的田野——
路那边，结冰的水塘
我的脚踩在冰面上。
它吱嘎作响
下面的白气
窜出，黑冰的
裂纹瞬间铺开
我这带钉的山地靴
打滑在坚硬溜滑的冰面上
——像薄冰——忽觉
一古语真真切切——
冻树叶、冰水和手中的
拐杖刹那翻个。
“如履薄冰——”

I yelled back to a friend,

It broke and I dropped

Eight inches in

我回头急喊同伴,

冰已破, 我掉进水中

八英寸

All Through the Rains

That mare stood in the field—

A big pine tree and a shed,

But she stayed in the open

Ass to the wind, splash wet.

I tried to catch her April

For a bareback ride,

She kicked and bolted

Later grazing fresh shoots

In the shade of the down

Eucalyptus on the hill.

雨中见

那匹母马伫立于田野——
附近一棵大松树和一间马棚，
但她待在露天之处
屁股迎风，被溅湿。
四月我曾想抓住她
骑上她的光背，
她尥蹶子，奔逃而去
后来在山上倒下的
桉树树影中
啃嚼嫩草。

Tōji

Shingon Temple, Kyoto

Men asleep in their underwear
Newspapers under their heads
Under the eaves of Tōji,
Kobo Daishi solid iron and ten feet tall
Strides through, a pigeon on his hat.

Peering through chickenwire grates
At dusty gold-leaf statues
A cynical curving round-belly
Cool Bodhisattva—maybe Avalokita—
Bisexual and tried it all, weight on
One leg, haloed in snake-hood gold
Shines through the shadow

东寺[1]

真言宗寺庙，京都

东寺屋檐下
穿短裤睡觉的男人们
头枕报纸，
十英尺高的弘法大师[2]铁骨铮铮
大步走过，一只鸽子栖在帽顶。

透过鸡笼窗格
瞥见积尘的金叶上的塑像
一尊佛[3]，浑圆的肚子
玩世而淡定——也许是菩萨[4]——
双性兼修，一条腿
撑住重心，金背光形如蛇的瘪颈
灿然于暗影

1 东寺，日本京都古寺。

2 弘法大师 (774—835)，本名空海，日本僧人。

3 原文 Bodhisattva，菩萨。

4 原文 Avalokita，观世音菩萨。

An ancient hip smile
Tingling of India and Tibet.

Loose-breasted young mother
With her kids in the shade here
Of old Temple tree,
Nobody bothers you in Tōji;
The streetcar clanks by outside.

一种古老的嬉皮微笑
袭来印度和西藏

这里，古寺的树影中
乳房松垂的年轻母亲
看着她的孩子们，
在东寺你无人打扰；
寺外有街车哐哐驶过。

Kyoto: March

A few light flakes of snow
Fall in the feeble sun;
Birds sing in the cold,
A warbler by the wall. The plum
Buds tight and chill soon bloom.
The moon begins first
Fourth, a faint slice west
At nightfall. Jupiter half-way
High at the end of night-
Meditation. The dove cry
Twangs like a bow.
At dawn Mt. Hiei dusted white
On top; in the clear air
Folds of all the gullied green
Hills around the town are sharp,
Breath stings. Beneath the roofs
Of frosty houses
Lovers part, from tangle warm
Of gentle bodies under quilt

京都：三月

几片轻盈的雪花
在虚弱的阳光中飘落；
寒意习习，众鸟歌唱，
墙畔鸣禽一只。李树的
花蕾冷缩着，就要开放。
四分之一个月亮
初露，暮色中西天淡淡的
一痕。走在中途的木星
高悬于夜间冥想
结束之际。鸽子鸣叫
如琴弓触弦。
黎明时分比睿山山顶
白茫茫一片；空气清澈
镇子周围所有绿色山岗的
沟谷棱角分明，
呼吸凛冽。霜冻的
屋顶下面
相爱者分开，离开被窝里
轻柔躯体缠绵的温暖

And crack the icy water to the face
And wake and feed the children
And grandchildren that they love.

用冰水扑脸
醒透，然后给他们所爱的
儿孙们做早饭。

Goofing Again

Goofing again
I shifted weight the wrong way
flipping the plank end-over
dumping me down in the bilge
& splatting a gallon can
of thick sticky dark red
italian deck paint
over the fresh white bulkhead.
such a trifling move
& such spectacular results.
now I have to paint the wall again
& salvage only from it all a poem.

又蠢一回

又蠢一回

我移错位置，重力失衡

踩得木板撅起

把我肚子朝下掼倒在地

并把罐装一加仑

又稠又黏的意大利

深红色甲板漆

刮涂上爽白的挡土墙

这么一小步挪移

这么晕菜的后果。

我现在不得不重新刷墙

只从中捞出一首诗。

Riprap

Lay down these words
Before your mind like rocks.
    placed solid, by hands
In choice of place, set
Before the body of the mind
    in space and time:
Solidity of bark, leaf, or wall
    riprap of things:
Cobble of milky way,
    straying planets,
These poems, people,
    lost ponies with
Dragging saddles
    and rocky sure-foot trails.
The worlds like an endless
    four-dimensional
Game of Go.
    ants and pebbles
In the thin loam, each rock a word
    a creek-washed stone

砌石

码放好这些词语
在你的心灵变得像岩石之前。
　　选定位置的双手，将它们
牢牢放好，放在
心灵的躯体面前
　　在空间和时间里：
树皮、树叶或墙壁的结实
　　事物的码嵌：
银河里的圆石
　　漂泊的行星，
这些诗，这些人，
　　拖着鞍鞯的
丢失的小马
　　以及岩石上确定的足迹。
诸世界像一盘无限大的
　　四维空间的
围棋游戏。
　　蚂蚁和卵石
在薄土之中，一石即一词
　　一块被溪水冲刷的石头

Granite: ingrained

with torment of fire and weight

Crystal and sediment linked hot

all change, in thoughts,

As well as things.

花岗岩：被整塑于

　　火与重量的折磨

晶体和沉积层热结在一起

　　全在变，在思想之中，

也在事物之中。

Once Only

almost at the equator
almost at the equinox
exactly at midnight
from a ship
the full

moon

in the center of the sky.

Sappa Creek near Singapore
March 1958

只一次

几乎在赤道
几乎在秋分时
恰子夜时分
船头望
满

月

天宇正中央

新加坡附近萨帕溪

1958年3月

After Work

The shack and a few trees
float in the blowing fog

I pull out your blouse,
warm my cold hands
        on your breasts.
you laugh and shudder
peeling garlic by the
        hot iron stove.
bring in the axe, the rake,
the wood

We'll lean on the wall
against each other
stew simmering on the fire
as it grows dark
        drinking wine.

收工以后

流动的雾裹挟着
小木屋和树木几株

我褪下你的罩衫，
在你的乳房上
　　暖我的凉手。
你笑，你颤抖
在热铁炉子旁
　　剥蒜皮。
带进来斧子、耙子，
和木头

我们将面对面
靠在墙上
天黑下来
火上炖着东西
　　喝酒。

The Public Bath

the bath-girl

getting dressed, in the mirror,
the bath-girl with a pretty mole and a
red skirt is watching me:
am I
different?

the baby boy

on his back, dashed with scalding water
silent, moving eyes
inscrutably
pees.

the daughters

gripping and scrubbing his two little daughters
they squirm, shriek at
soap-in-the-eye,

公共浴池

洗澡的姑娘

穿衣，在镜中
　　这洗澡的姑娘长一颗好看的痣
穿件红衬衫，看着我
　　我有什么
　　　　不同吗？

小男孩

仰躺着，手劈热水
安静，眼睛转动
不可思议地
尿尿。

女儿们

他攥着他的两个小女儿给她们擦洗
　　她们扭动，为眼睛里进了肥皂沫
　　　　而尖叫，

wring out their own hair
with grave wifely hands,
peek at me, point, while he
soaps up and washes their
plump little tight-lip pussies
peers in their ears,
& dunks them in hot tile tub.
with a brown-burnt farmboy
a shrivelled old man
and a student who sings silent night.

—we waver and float like seaweed
pink flesh in the steamy light.

the old woman

too fat and too old to care
she just stands there
idly knocking dewy water off her
bush.

the young woman

gazing vacant, drying her neck

却以妇人的动作

　　拧干自己的头发，

偷看我，指点，当男人给自己

打满肥皂并给她们洗那

　　肥嘟嘟紧收着的小屁屁

并在她们耳边低语

　　然后把她们扔进铺瓷砖的热水浴池。

　　浴池中泡着一个紫铜色的农家小子

　　一个干瘦的老头

　　一个唱着《平安夜》的学生

——我们像水草一样舞动，随波逐流

白亮的蒸汽中粉红色的肉体。

老妇人

太胖太老不惹眼

　她就站在那里

　　有一搭无一搭地拨拉掉她阴毛上的

　　　水滴

年轻女人

目中茫然，擦干她的脖子

faint fuzz of hair
little points of breasts
—next year she'll be dressing
out of sight.

the men

squatting soapy and limber
smooth dense skin, long muscles—

I see dead men naked
tumbled on beaches
newsreels, the
war

头发下的小细毛

小乳头

——明年她将梳妆打扮

超好看。

男人们

弹性的肢体，一身肥皂泡蹲着

光滑的绷紧的皮肤，长条肌肉——

我看到死去的男人们赤裸

翻倒在海滩上

新闻短片，

战争

Four Poems for Robin

Siwashing it out once in Siuslaw Forest

I slept under rhododendron
All night blossoms fell
Shivering on a sheet of cardboard
Feet stuck in my pack
Hands deep in my pockets
Barely able to sleep.
I remembered when we were in school
Sleeping together in a big warm bed
We were the youngest lovers
When we broke up we were still nineteen.
Now our friends are married
You teach school back east
I don't mind living this way
Green hills the long blue beach
But sometimes sleeping in the open
I think back when I had you.

给罗宾的四首诗

像塞瓦什人一样露宿在休斯洛森林[1]

我睡在　杜鹃花下
整夜　花瓣落着
颤抖在　一片纸箱板上
双脚伸进　我的背包
双手插在　我的兜里
刚好　可以　入睡。
我记得　那时在学校
在一张温暖的大床上　我们睡在一起
我们是　最小的恋人
分手时　我们才只有十九岁。
现在朋友们　都已结婚
你已回到东部　在学校教书
我不在乎　如此生活
青山　长长的蓝色海滩
但有时　睡在露天
我回想起　有你的日子。

1　塞瓦什人系北美太平洋沿岸一印第安部落。休斯洛森林位于美国俄勒冈州。

*

A spring night in Shokoku-ji

Eight years ago this May
We walked under cherry blossoms
At night in an orchard in Oregon.
All that I wanted then
Is forgotten now, but you.
Here in the night
In a garden of the old capital
I feel the trembling ghost of Yugao
I remember your cool body
Naked under a summer cotton dress.

*

An autumn morning in Shokoku-ji

Last night watching the Pleiades,
Breath smoking in the moonlight,

*

春夜在相国寺[1]

八年前的这个五月
在俄勒冈的夜晚的果园
我们漫步在樱树花下。
那时我想要的一切
如今都已忘记，除了你。
这里，在一座古都的
花园的夜晚
我感受到夕颜[2]颤抖的鬼魂
我记得你凉凉的身体
裸赤在棉布夏装之内。

*

秋晨在相国寺

昨夜仰望昴宿七星，
月色中哈气成雾，

1 相国寺是一座临济宗寺庙，位于日本京都北部。

2 夕颜，日本紫式部小说《源氏物语》中的角色。

Bitter memory like vomit
Choked my throat.
I unrolled a sleeping bag
On mats on the porch
Under thick autumn stars.
In dream you appeared
(Three times in nine years)
Wild, cold, and accusing.
I woke shamed and angry:
The pointless wars of the heart.
Almost dawn. Venus and Jupiter.
The first time I have
Ever seen them close.

*

December at Yase

You said, that October,
In the tall dry grass by the orchard
When you chose to be free,
"Again someday, maybe ten years."

苦涩的记忆如呕吐
堵住我的喉咙。
在门廊的垫子上
我摊开睡袋
秋夜星辰密布
你来到我的梦中
（九年里出现了三次）
野性，冷淡，指责我。
我醒来惭愧而愤怒：
我们两颗心间无意义的战争。
黎明将至，金星和木星。
我还是第一次看到
它们相距如此之近。

*

十二月在八濑[1]

那年十月，
在果园深深的干草丛中，
在你选择了自由的时候，你说
“哪天再会，也许十年以后”。

1 八濑，京都地名。

After college I saw you
One time. You were strange.
And I was obsessed with a plan.

Now ten years and more have
Gone by: I've always known
    where you were—
I might have gone to you
Hoping to win your love back.
You still are single.

I didn't.
I thought I must make it alone. I
Have done that.

Only in dream, like this dawn,
Does the grave, awed intensity
Of our young love
Return to my mind, to my flesh.

We had what the others
All crave and seek for;
We left it behind at nineteen.

大学以后我看见你
一回。你怪样子。
而我正为一个计划而着迷。

现在十多年
已经过去：我一直知道
　　你在哪里——
我本可以去找你
以便挽回你的爱
你依然单身。

我没去。
我想我必须一个人干，我
就是这样做的。

只在梦中，像在这个黎明
我们年轻时恋爱的
严肃、敬畏的紧张
回到我的脑海、我的肉体。

别人贪求和寻找的东西
我们曾经拥有；
但我们抛弃了它，在十九岁上。

I feel ancient, as though I had
Lived many lives.

And may never now know
If I am a fool
Or have done what my
　　karma demands.

我感到自身古老，好像曾
活过多次。

最好永不知道
我是否一个傻瓜
或者我所做的
　　全是业报因果。

The Firing

for Les Blakebrough and the memory of John Chappell

Bitter blue fingers
Winter nineteen sixty-three A.D.
    showa thirty-eight
Over a low pine-covered splay of hills in Shiga
West-south-west of the outlet of Lake Biwa
Domura village set on sandy fans of the sweep
    and turn of a river
Draining the rotten-granite hills up Shigaraki
On a nineteen-fifty-seven Honda cycle model C
Rode with some Yamanashi wine "St Neige"
Into the farmyard and the bellowing kiln.
Les & John
In ragged shirts and pants, dried slip
Stuck to with pineneedle, pitch,
    dust, hair, woodchips;
Sending the final slivers of yellowy pine

烧窑

为莱丝·布莱克布劳而作并怀念约翰·查佩尔

苦涩的黑手指
公元一九六三年冬
　　昭和三十八年
在滋贺县松林覆盖的低矮的山丘坡地
琵琶湖西南偏西的湖滨
土村，位于河流拐弯处
多沙的冲积扇
河流将花岗岩砂浆带向信乐[1]
莱丝和约翰
骑一辆一九五七年 C 型本田摩托
驮着些山梨县产圣涅日葡萄酒
驶入农家院和下面的瓷窑。
他们破裤烂衫，因为摔了大跟头
衣服上扎着松针，粘着树脂
　　尘土、毛发、木屑；
他们通过白炽喷热的窥火孔

1　信乐，日本六大古窑之一信乐烧的故乡。

Through peephole white blast glow
No saggars tilting yet and segers bending
    neatly in a row—
Even their beards caked up with mud & soot
Firing for fourteen hours. How does she go.
Porcelain & stoneware: cheese dish, twenty cups.
Tokuri. vases. black chawan
Crosslegged rest on the dirt eye cockt to smoke—

The hands you layed on clay
Kickwheeld, curling,
    creamed to the lip of nothing,
And coaxt to a white dancing heat that day
Will linger centuries in these towns and loams
And speak to men or beasts
When Japanese and English
Are dead tongues.

投入最后的一条条发黄的松木

耐火匣钵尚未倾斜，测温棒弯曲

　　整齐地排列——

窑已烧过十四小时，连他们的胡子

都与泥巴烟灰板结成块。窑炉会怎样。

瓷器和粗陶器：奶酪盘，二十个杯子，

胆瓶。花瓶。黑茶碗。

两人盘腿歇在又脏又乱的地上，眼睛被烟呛红——

你们留在经拉坯旋转的

胎泥上的弧形手痕

　　浑然化入陶碗的空无之唇，

并哄出那一日舞动的白色热气，

你们的手痕将逡巡于这一带的城镇和沃土

对人和野兽说话

当日语和英语

已经变成死去的语言。

Mother of the Buddhas, Queen of Heaven, Mother of the Sun; Marici, Goddess of the Dawn

for Bhikku Ghosananda

old sow in the mud
bristles caked black
down her powerful neck

tiny hooves churn
squat body slithering
deep in food dirt

her warm filth,
deep-plowing snout,
dragging teats

those who keep her

佛母，天后，太阳之母；摩利支天[1]，黎明女神

为比库·高萨南达而作

烂泥中的老母猪
粗壮的脖子上
黑鬃硬结

小猪蹄蹬踹
蹲伏的身躯沉入
脏臭的泔水

她那温暖的污秽，
深耕的猪鼻子
拖着奶头

那些养她

1 摩利支天，梵语 Marici，也作具光佛母、光明佛母等。摩利支天也被印度教与道教所信奉，道教称作斗姥、斗姆、斗母等。密宗中摩利支天是观音菩萨的化身，具有隐形之术，时常暗中护持信徒，救人厄难。在佛寺的造像一般是一天女形象，手持莲花，头顶宝塔，坐骑是金豕。

or eat her

are cast out

she turns her small eye

from earth to

look up at me.

Nalanda, Bihar

或吃她的人

被驱逐

她从地上

撩起她的小眼睛

看我

纳烂陀，比哈尔

For John Chappell

1964

Over the Arafura sea, the China sea,
    Coral sea, Pacific
chains of volcanoes in the dark—
you in Sydney where it's summer;
I imagine that last ride outward
late at night.
        stiff new gears—tight new engine
up some highway I have never seen
too fast—too fast—
    like I said at Tango
    when you went down twice on gravel—

Did you have a chance to think
o shit I've fucked it now
instant crash and flight and sudden death—

为约翰·查佩尔而作

1964

阿拉弗拉海、中国海、
　　珊瑚海、太平洋之上
黑暗中的火山之链——
你在正值夏季的悉尼；
我想象你最后一次骑摩托出门
在深夜。
　　　锃新的传动齿轮——簇新的发动机
骑上某条我从未见过的公路
太快了——太快了——
　　像我在丹后山[1]说过的那样
　　当时你两次冲下沙砾之路——

你是否还来得及想
妈的我死定了
瞬间撞毁，飞起，突然死亡——

1　丹后山，日本地名。

Malaya, Indonesia
Taiwan, the Philippines, Okinawa
families sleeping—reaching—
humans by the millions
world of breathing flesh.

me in Kyoto. You in Australia
wasted in the night.
black beard, mad laugh, and sadly serious brow.
earth lover, shaper and maker.
potter, cooker,

now be clay in the ground.

马来亚、印度尼西亚
台湾、菲律宾、冲绳
　　合家入眠——睡梦伸展——
　　千千人万万人
　　呼吸着的肉体的世界。

我在京都。你在澳大利亚
烂醉如泥在夜晚。
黑胡子，狂笑，忧戚的眉毛。
　大地的恋人，塑造者和创造者。
　　制陶工，厨子，

　现在入土为泥。

Twelve Hours Out of New York After Twenty-Five Days at Sea

The sun always setting behind us.
I did not mean to come this far.
    —baseball games on the radio
    commercials that turn your hair—
The last time I sailed this coast
Was nineteen forty eight
Washing galley dishes
    reading Gide in French.
In the rucksack I've got three nata
Handaxes from central Japan;
The square blade found in China
    all the way back to Stone—
A novel by Kafu NAGAI
About geisha in nineteen-ten
With a long thing about gardens
And how they change through the year;
Azalea ought to be blooming
    in the yard in Kyoto now.

航海二十五日后距纽约城十二小时

太阳总在我们背后落下。

我没想到会走这么远。

　　——广播里播放着棒球比赛

　　让你回头的染发广告——

上回我航行到这一带海岸

是在一九四八年

在船上餐厅洗盘子

　　读法语的纪德。

帆布背包里带着三把铊刀

来自日本中部的手斧；

在中国找到的石钺

　　一直可以追溯到石器时代——

一部永井荷风[1]的长篇小说

关于一九一〇年的艺妓

其中有关于花园的大段描写

一年中植物如何枯荣；

此刻杜鹃花当开放于

　　京都的庭院。

1　永井荷风（1879—1959），日本唯美派代表作家。

Now we are north of Cape Hatteras

Tomorrow docking at eight.

    mop the deck round the steering gear,

Pack your stuff and get paid.

19 IV 64

此刻我们行至海特拉斯角之北
明天将在八点下碇。
　　清洗舵机周围的甲板
收拾好你的东西，领钱。

19 IV 64

In the House of the Rising Sun

Skinny kids in shorts get cups
    full of rice-gruel—steaming
    breakfast—sling
    their rifles, walk
    hot thickets.
    eyes peeled for U S planes.

Kyoto a bar girl in pink
    with her catch for the night
    —but it's already morning—half-
    dazed, neat suit,
    laugh toward bed,

A guy I worked at logging with in Oregon
    fiddles his new lead-belcher cannons
        in South Yüeh.
    tuned better than chainsaws,
        at dawn,

在日出之家[1]

穿短裤的小孩子们皮包骨，接过
　　盛满米粥的粥碗——这冒着热气的
　　早饭——他们挎着
　　步枪，行走在
　　闷热的灌木丛中
　　眼睛警惕地搜寻美国飞机

京都　一个穿粉衣的酒吧女郎
　　与她钓到的混夜男孩在一起
　　——但已天亮——他有些
　　头晕眼花，但衣装整洁，
　　边笑边走到床边，

一个曾与我一起在俄勒冈伐木场干活的小伙子
　　　　在南越
　　弄着他崭新的打嗝的加农炮。
　　音色强于链锯的切割声，
　　　　黎明时分

1　日本有“日出之家”之称。同时美国新奥尔良曾有一家妓院名为“日出之家”。此或为双关语。

he liked mush.   with raisins.

Sleeping out all night

in warm rain.

Viet Nam uplands burned-off jungles

wipe out a few rare birds

Fish in the rice paddy ditches

stream a dry foul taste thru their gills

New Asian strains of clap

whip penic   ill in.

Making toast, heating coffee,

blue as Shiva—

did I drink some filthy poison

will I ever learn to love?

Did I really have to kill my sick, sick cat.

他喜欢喝稀饭。带葡萄干的那一种。

整夜　在暖雨中

睡在外面。

越南丘陵地区焚毁的丛林

消灭了几种稀缺的鸟类

鱼游在稻田的沟壑里

双腮翕张习惯了脏水

亚洲新型的淋病变种

不在乎盘尼　戏　淋。[1]

烤面包，煮咖啡

黑如湿婆[2]——

我是否喝下了肮脏的毒药

我是否曾经学过爱？

我是否真得杀死我生病的，生病的猫。

1　原文 penic ill in 拆自 penicillin（盘尼西林）。作者在此玩弄词汇，使药品盘尼西林获得了“病入”(ill in) 的意思。

2　原文 blue as Shiva。但湿婆并不以黑肤色著称。在印度宗教神话中以黑肤色著称的是毗湿奴的转生克里希那，另译黑天。

Kyoto Born in Spring Song

Beautiful little children
　　found in melons,
　　in bamboo,
　in a "strangely glowing warbler egg"
　　a perfect baby girl—

baby, baby,
　tiny precious
　　mice and worms:

　Great majesty of Dharma turning
　Great dance of Vajra power

lizard baby by the fern
centipede baby scrambling toward the wall
cat baby left to mew for milk alone
mouse baby too afraid to run

　　O sing　born in spring

京都诞生于春日之歌

美丽的小孩们
　　诞生在瓜果中，
　　竹子中，
　一只“奇怪闪光的鸟蛋”里
　　蹦出个漂亮的女娃娃——

娃娃，娃娃
　细小珍贵的
　　老鼠和虫子：

　伟大的殊胜佛法运作
　伟大的金刚之力舞蹈

蜥蜴团团隐伏于蕨丛
蜈蚣团团爬向墙边
被关笼中的猫团团自己喝奶
胆子太小的鼠团团不敢跑动

　　哦　歌唱　生于春日

the weavers swallows babies in Nishijin
nests below the eaves

glinting mothers wings
swoop to the sound of looms

and three fat babies
with three human mothers
every morning doing laundry
"good
morning how's your baby?"
Tomoharu, Itsuko, and Kenji—

Mouse, begin again.

Bushmen are laughing
at the coyote-tricking
that made us think machines

wild babies
in the ferns and plums and weeds.

西阵[1]织巢燕子的团团
住在屋檐之下

燕子母亲们闪光的翅膀扑扇，飞冲
伴着织机的声响

三位人类母亲
带着三个胖娃娃
每天早晨洗衣裳
"早上好
你的娃娃怎么样？"
友治、伊都子，还有见次——

老鼠，再一次开始。

丛林人在为施诡计
捕到土狼而大笑
这令我们想到机械

蕨丛、李树和草丛中的
小动物。

1 西阵，日本地名。

Burning Island

O Wave God who broke through me today
Sea Bream
massive pink and silver
cool swimming down with me watching
staying away from the spear

Volcano belly Keeper who lifted this island
for our own beaded bodies adornment
and sprinkles us all with his laugh—
ash in the eye
mist, or smoke,
on the bare high limits—
underwater lava flows easing to coral
holes filled with striped feeding swimmers

O Sky Gods cartwheeling
out of Pacific
turning rainsqualls over like lids on us
then shine on our sodden—

火烧岛

哦　波浪之神　今天是谁将我贯穿
　　大海真鲷
　　粉红和银灰的鱼群巨阵
　　随我俊然下潜，观察着
　　　　避开矛叉

火山腹部的守护者，为我们
　　挂着饰珠的躯体
　　举起这岛屿
　　并向我们喷淋他的大笑——
　　　　满眼灰烬
　　光秃的礁石高出水面，石顶
　　被雾绕烟封——
　　　而水下熔岩自在流向
　　　　挤满觅食斑纹鱼的珊瑚洞

哦　天空之神　车轮般
　　升起于　太平洋
　　在我们头顶旋开盖子般的暴风雨
　　然后照耀透湿的我们——

(scanned out a rainbow today at the
cow drinking trough
sluicing off
LAKHS of crystal Buddha Fields
right on the hair of the arm!)

Who wavers right now in the bamboo:
a half-gone waning moon.
drank down a bowlful of shochu
in praise of Antares
gazing far up the lanes of Sagittarius
richest stream of our sky—
a cup to the center of the galaxy!
and let the eyes stray
right-angling the pitch of the Milky Way:
horse-heads   rings
clouds   too distant to be
slide free.
on the crest of the wave.

（描出今日的彩虹

跨在饮牛的水槽上

开闸放水

灌溉数十万[1]亩佛陀水晶的田野

恰在臂膀的汗毛上！）

此刻谁在竹丛中摇闪：

一轮半隐的苍白的月亮。

喝下一碗烧酒[2]

赞美心宿二[3]

凝眺遥远的人马座小巷

我们天上最丰富的溪流——

为银河系的核心干一杯！

并让眼睛移动

视线直角顶抵银河的最高处：

马头　指环

云朵　太远了

不能自由滑动。

在浪峰之上。

1　作者此处使用的是佛教用语 Lakh，即十万。

2　原文 shochu，指日本烧酒。

3　原文 Antares，指天蝎座 α 星。中国古代又称大火，心宿二。

Each night
O Earth Mother
    I have wrappt my hand
    over the jut of your cobra-hood
                    sleeping;
    left my ear
All night long by your mouth.

O   All
Gods   tides   capes   currents
Flows and spirals of
    pool and powers—

As we hoe the field
    let sweet potato grow.
And as sit us all down when we may
To consider the Dharma
    bring with a flower and a glimmer.
Let us all sleep in peace   together.

Bless Masa and me as we marry
    at new moon   on the crater
This summer.

VIII 40067

每夜

哦　大地母亲

　　在你眼镜蛇般的睡眠中

　　我用手捂住你的

　　　　耸立的部位

　　将我的耳朵

整夜靠在你的嘴边

哦　一切

神明　潮汐　海角　洋流

水潭和力的

　　涌流与盘转——

当我们耕作于田野

　　愿甜薯生长。

当我们可以坐下时让我们坐下

思索佛法，或达摩

　　带来的一朵花和一道亮光。

愿我们全部安睡　在一起。

祝福玛萨和我，我们在

　　新月下结婚　在火山口

在这个夏天。

VIII 40067

Rainbow Body

Cicada fill up the bamboo thickets:
a wall of twanging shadow
dark joints and leaves.
northwest wind
from the China sea.

Salt clouds skim the volcano
mixed with ash and steam
rumbles downwind
from the night gleam
summit, near Algol,
breathing the Milky Way.

The great drone
In the throat of the hill
The waves drum
The wind sigh.

At dawn the mountain canyons
spread and rise

彩虹身躯

蝉满竹丛：

　　一道蝉噪的阴影之墙

　　　　幽暗的缠结和竹叶。

　　　　　　来自中国海的

　　　　西北风。

混杂着灰烬和水蒸气的

　　盐之云掠过火山

　　　　顺着风，自靠近阿果的

　　　　　　夜晚闪烁的峰顶

　　　　隆隆而下

　　呼吸着银河的气息。

山岭的喉咙里

巨大的嗡鸣

海浪的鼓声

风的叹息。

黎明时分山谷

　　展开并升起

to the falling call of the Akahige
we half-wake
in the east light
fresh

At low tide swim out through a path in the coral
& into the land of the sea-people:
rainbows under the foam of the breakers
surge and streaming
from the southern beach.
the lips, where you float
clear, wave
with the subtle currents
sea-tangle tendrils
outward roil of lava
—cobalt speckled curling
mouth of a shako clam.

Climb delicately back up the cliff
without using our hands.
eat melon and steamed sweet potato
from this ground.
We hoed and fished—

回应着鹌鸟降下的召唤

我们半醒

在东方破晓之光里

清新一派

小小的涨潮，游过珊瑚之路

进入海洋人民的土地：

在闯入者搅起的浪沫下面

来自南岸的彩虹躯体

汹涌游动

你所漂之处，蛤喇唇

清爽，举起波浪的

是微妙的水流

这大海翻滚的鬆须

火山熔岩外射的浊流

——斑点遍布的钴蓝色的扭曲岩石

一只虾蛄的嘴。

不用手攀手扶

我们优美地爬回悬崖。

吃瓜和本地产的

蒸红薯。

我们耕地打鱼——

grubbing out bamboo runners

hammering straight blunt

harpoon heads and spears

        Now,

sleep on the cliff

float on the surf

nap in the bamboo thicket

      eyes closed,

dazzled ears.

挖出带须的竹根

将磨钝弯曲的鱼叉头和长矛头

敲直磨利

　　现在,

睡在悬崖上

出没于浪峰波谷

小憩在竹丛里

　　闭上眼,

满耳精彩。

Everybody Lying on Their Stomachs, Head Toward the Candle, Reading, Sleeping, Drawing

The corrugated roof
Booms and fades night-long to

                    million-darted rain
            squalls and

                    outside

                    lightning

Photographs in the brain
Wind-bent bamboo.
                         through

                    the plank shutter
                         set

Half-open   on eternity

人人卧着，头向烛光，读书，
睡觉，画画

起伏的屋顶
轰轰作响，彻夜隐身于

急落的万千雨箭
呼啸着　而

门外

是电闪

脑海中的画面
风中弯腰的竹子。
透过

半开的　木板
窗扇

向着永恒

Shark Meat

In the night fouled the nets—
Sonoyama's flying-fish fishing
Speared by the giant trident
          that hung in the net shed
                    we never thought used

Cut up for meat on the beach.
At seven in the morning
Maeda's grandson
                              the shy one
                    —a slight harelip
Brought a crescent of pale red flesh
          two feet long, looped on his arm
Up the bamboo lanes to our place.

The island eats shark meat at noon.
Sweet miso sauce on a big boiled cube
          as I lift a flake

鲨鱼肉

夜间，渔网缠绞——
园山[1]假饵捕鱼
用挂在渔网工棚的
　　巨大的三头鱼叉刺戳
　　　　我们从未想过要用到它

在岸边割下肉
早七点
前田的孙子
　　　　　　那害羞的男孩
　　　　——有点儿兔唇
胳膊上搭着新月形的
　　淡红色的肉，两英尺长
沿竹篁小径来到我们的住处。

岛上人中午吃鲨鱼肉。
甜豆面酱浇在煮熟的大肉块上
　　我夹起一片

1　园山系当地小渔村村长的姓氏。

to my lips,

Miles of water, Black current,
Thousands of days
    re-crossing his own paths
    to tangle our net
        to be part of
        this loom.

到唇边，

海上，数英里远，黑色的水流，
成千个日夜
鲨鱼之路
再次与我们的渔网相绞
成为这织机的
一部分

Revolution in the Revolution in the Revolution

The country surrounds the city
The back country surrounds the country

"From the masses to the masses" the most
Revolutionary consciousness is to be found
Among the most ruthlessly exploited classes:
Animals, trees, water, air, grasses

We must pass through the stage of the
"Dictatorship of the Unconscious" before we can
Hope for the withering-away of the states
And finally arrive at true Communionism.

*

If the capitalists and imperialists
        are the exploiters, the masses are the workers.
                and the party
                is the communist.

革命中的革命中的革命

乡村环绕着城市
落后的乡村环绕着乡村

“从大众到大众”最高的
革命觉悟应该存在于
那些被最残酷剥削的阶级之中：
动物、树木、水、空气、野草

在我们可以期望国家凋亡
并最终抵达共享主义之前
我们必须越过
“无意识独裁”的阶段。

*

如果资本家和帝国主义者们
　　是剥削者，大众就是劳动者。
　　　　而党
　　　　就是共产主义者。

If civilization

    is the exploiter, the masses is nature.

        and the party

        is the poets.

If the abstract rational intellect

    is the exploiter, the masses is the unconscious.

        and the party

        is the yogins.

& POWER

comes out of the seed-syllables of mantras.

如果文明

　　是剥削者，大众就是自然。

　　　　而党

　　　　就是诗人。

如果抽象的理性智力

　　是剥削者，大众就是无意识。

　　　　而党

　　　　就是瑜伽师。

而力量

来自曼陀罗的种子音节[1]。

1　梵文中称种子音节为 bija，构成咒语或颂歌。例如 Om Ah Hum 即种子音节：Om 唤起“合一”的意识；Ah 唤起“语言、知识”；Hum 唤起“实现”。它们分别来自头脑、喉咙和身心。

Meeting the Mountains

He crawls to the edge of the foaming creek
He backs up the slab ledge
He puts a finger in the water
He turns to a trapped pool
Puts both hands in the water
Puts one foot in the pool
Drops pebbles in the pool
He slaps the water surface with both hands
He cries out, rises up and stands
Facing toward the torrent and the mountain
Raises up both hands and shouts three times!

VI 69, Kai at Sawmill Lake

与群山相会

他爬到翻着泡沫的山溪边

他退向探出的巨石

他向水中探出一个手指

他转身走向一个积水的深潭

将双手探进水中

将一只脚伸进潭中

向潭中扔石头

他用双手拍打水面

他喊一声，起身，站定

面向急流和山峦

举起双手，高呼三次！

开[1]在索密尔湖，VI 69

---

1 开 Kai，盖瑞 · 施耐德的儿子。

Pine Tree Tops

in the blue night

frost haze, the sky glows

with the moon

pine tree tops

bend snow-blue, fade

into sky, frost, starlight.

the creak of boots.

rabbit tracks, deer tracks,

what do we know.

松冠

蓝色的夜
霜霭，空中
明月朗照
雪之蓝令松冠
弯垂，融入
天空，白霜，星光。
靴子的吱嘎声。
兔踪、鹿迹，
我们知道什么。

Night Herons

Night herons nest in the cypress
by the San Francisco
stationary boilers
with the high smoke stack
at the edge of the waters:
a steam turbine pump
to drive salt water
into the city's veins
mains
if the earth ever
quakes. and the power fails.
and water
to fight fire, runs
loose on the streets
with no pressure.

At the wire gate tilted slightly out
the part-wolf dog
would go in, to follow
if his human buddy lay on his side

夜鹭

在旧金山水畔
在那竖着高大烟囱的
锅炉房一侧
夜鹭巢于柏树的枝冠：
一架蒸汽涡轮泵
将在地震时
抽海水输入城市的
大街小巷。停电了。
压力全无，救火的水
在街道上
四溢。

在铁艺篱笆微微外倾的小门旁
半是狼的狗
想跟主人进去
如果躺在他身旁的人类密友

and squirmed up first.

An abandoned, decaying, army.
a rotten rusty island prison
surrounded by lights of whirling
fluttering god-like birds
who truth
has never forgot.

I walk with my wife's sister
past the frozen bait;
with a long-bearded architect,
my dear brother,
and silent friend, whose
mustache curves wetly into his mouth
and he sometimes bites it.

the dog knows no laws and is strictly,
illegal. His neck arches and ears prick out
to catch mice in the tundra
a black high school boy
drinking coffee at a fake green stand
tries to be friends with the dog,

首先动弹。

一支被废弃的、朽坏的，军队。
一座生锈的岛屿监狱
周围是鼓翼飞旋的
神一般的鸟雀
其真理
从未忘记。

我和我妻妹
走过一罐冻鱼饵；
身边是位胡子老长的建筑师，
我亲爱的兄弟，
和安静的朋友，他有时
咬咬湿湿地
弯进嘴里的唇髭

狗不通法律，严格说来，
是非法的。他拱着脖子，耳朵竖起
警惕着冻土上的老鼠。
一个黑孩儿，高中生
在一个歪斜的绿架摊子前喝咖啡
逗狗，想和他交朋友，

and it works.

How could the
night herons ever come back?
to this noisy place on the bay.
like me.
the joy of all the beings
is in being
older and tougher and eaten
up.
in the tubes and lanes of things
in the sewers of bliss and judgment,
in the glorious cleansing
treatment
plants.

We pick our way
through the edge of the city
early
subtly spreading changing sky;

ever-fresh and lovely dawn.

真就交上了朋友

夜鹭
如何回到这里？
回到海湾这喧嚣之地。
像我。
所有生灵的乐趣
就在于
变老变硬被吃
光。
在事物的管径中
在福佑和审判的下水道中，
在光荣纯净的
疗伤的
植物中。

我们取道
穿过城市的边缘
早早的
微妙展开的变化的天空；

常新的可爱的黎明。

Mother Earth: Her Whales

An owl winks in the shadows
A lizard lifts on tiptoe, breathing hard
Young male sparrow stretches up his neck,
            big head, watching—

The grasses are working in the sun. Turn it green.
Turn it sweet. That we may eat.
Grow our meat.

Brazil says "sovereign use of Natural Resources"
Thirty thousand kinds of unknown plants.
The living actual people of the jungle
      sold and tortured—
And a robot in a suit who peddles a delusion called "Brazil"
      can speak for them?

The whales turn and glisten, plunge
      and sound and rise again,
Hanging over subtly darkening deeps
Flowing like breathing planets

母亲大地：她的鲸鱼们

阴影中一只猫头鹰眨眼
一只蜥蜴踮起脚尖，深呼吸
幼小的公麻雀高扬起脖子，
　　　　大脑袋，观望——

草类在太阳下工作。变绿。
变甜。给我们吃。
长我们的肉。

巴西说法“自然资源的主权使用”
三万种未知的植物。
真正的丛林居民
　　被贩卖，被折磨——
一个穿制服的机器人叫卖一个名唤“巴西”的错觉
　　能为他们说话？

鲸鱼们翻转，发光，跃回大海
　　发声，再跃起，
在窅暗的深海盘游
游动如呼吸的行星

in the sparkling whorls of
living light—

And Japan quibbles for words on
what kinds of whales they can kill?
A once-great Buddhist nation
dribbles methyl mercury
like gonorrhea
in the sea.

Père David's Deer, the Elaphure,
Lived in the tule marshes of the Yellow River
Two thousand years ago—and lost its home to rice—
The forests of Lo-yang were logged and all the silt &
Sand flowed down, and gone, by 1200 AD—

Wild Geese hatched out in Siberia
head south over basins of the Chiang, the Ho,
what we call "China"
On flyways they have used a million years.
Ah China, where are the tigers, the wild boars,
the monkeys,
like the snows of yesteryear

四周是闪烁跃动的

光的涡旋——

在何种鲸鱼可以捕杀的问题上

日本玩弄辞藻

一个曾经伟大的佛教国度

向大海滴注甲基汞

仿佛滴注淋病

病毒。

戴维王鹿，即厄拉弗大角鹿，

两千年前曾居于黄河两岸多草的沼泽

——其后被稻田夺去了家园——

洛阳的森林被砍伐，泥沙

下泻，被卷走，时在公元1200年——

大雁破壳于西伯利亚

循着百万年的鸟道

南飞越过长江黄河的诸盆地

我们称此地为“中国”

啊，中国，老虎们、野猪们、猴子们，

如去年的积雪

均去向何方

Gone in a mist, a flash, and the dry hard ground
Is parking space for fifty thousand trucks.
IS man most precious of all things?
—then let us love him, and his brothers, all those
Fading living beings—-

North America, Turtle Island, taken by invaders
        who wage war around the world.
May ants, may abalone, otters, wolves and elk
Rise! and pull away their giving
        from the robot nations.

Solidarity. The People.
Standing Tree People!
Flying Bird People!
Swimming Sea People!
Four-legged, two-legged people!

How can the head-heavy power-hungry politic scientist
Government   two-world   Capitalist-Imperialist
Third-world   Communist   paper-shuffling male
        non-farmer   jet-set   bureaucrats
Speak for the green of the leaf? Speak for the soil?

消失于迷雾和闪光，而干硬的土地
现在是五万辆卡车的停车场。
万物中人真的最珍贵？
——那就让我们爱他，和他的兄弟，那所有
正在逝去的生灵——

北美，龟岛，被入侵者占领
　　他们在全世界发动战争。
愿蚂蚁、鲍鱼、水獭、狼和麋鹿
起来！挣脱它们在
　　机器人国度的困境。

团结。人民。
站立之树的人民！
飞鸟的人民！
纵横海洋的人民！
四条腿的，两条腿的，人民！

那些头重脚轻、贪婪权力的政治学者
政府　　两个世界　　资本—帝国主义者
第三世界　共产主义者　文牍中的男人
　　非农户　打飞机的人　官僚们
他们怎会为叶子的绿色说话？为泥土说话？

(Ah Margaret Mead . . . do you sometimes dream of Samoa?)

The robots argue how to parcel out our Mother
    Earth
To last a little longer
        like vultures flapping
Belching, gurgling,
        near a dying Doe.

"In yonder field a slain knight lies—
We'll fly to him and eat his eyes
        with a down
    derry derry derry down down."

    An Owl winks in the shadow
A lizard lifts on tiptoe
        breathing hard
    The whales turn and glisten
        plunge and
    Sound, and rise again
    Flowing like breathing planets

（啊　玛格丽特·米德[1]……你会有时梦到萨摩亚吗？）

机器人争论如何分配我们的母亲大地
让她再活一小会儿
　　　　像秃鹰靠近将死的鹿
扇动翅膀，打嗝
　　　　嘴里发出咯咯的声音。

“在远方的田野躺着个骑士已身死——
我们飞到那里找到他
吃他的眼睛一口吞
　　好呀好呀一口吞呀一口吞。”

　　阴影中一只猫头鹰眨眼
一只蜥蜴踮起脚尖
　　　　深呼吸
　　鲸鱼们翻转，发光，
　　　　跃回大海
　　发声，再跃起，
　　在窅暗的深海盘游
　　游动如呼吸的行星

1　玛格丽特·米德（1901—1978），美国人类学家。

In the sparkling whorls

Of living light.

40072, Stockholm: Summer Solstice

四周是闪烁跃动的

光的涡旋。

40072，斯德哥尔摩：夏至

Tomorrow's Song

The USA slowly lost its mandate
in the middle and later twentieth century
it never gave the mountains and rivers,
          trees and animals,
                a vote.
all the people turned away from it
          myths die; even continents are impermanent

    Turtle Island returned.
    my friend broke open a dried coyote-scat
    removed a ground squirrel tooth
    pierced it, hung it
    from the gold ring
    in his ear.

We look to the future with pleasure
we need no fossil fuel
get power within
grow strong on less.

明日之歌

在二十世纪中期和后半叶
美国渐失其管理权
它从未给过山峦和河流
　　　　树木和动物，
　　　　　　选举权。
所有人背弃它
　　　　神话死去；即使大陆也只是暂存

　　龟岛回来了。
　　我的朋友砸开一头野狼的干尸
　　取出一颗地松鼠的牙齿
　　打孔，将它挂在
　　穿耳的
　　金耳环上。

我们欢乐地寄望于未来
我们不需要矿物燃料
获取内力
占有得更少而变强。

Grasp the tools and move in rhythm side by side
flash gleams of wit and silent knowledge
eye to eye
sit still like cats or snakes or stones
as whole and holding as
the blue black sky.
gentle and innocent as wolves
as tricky as a prince.
At work and in our place:

in the service
of the wilderness
of life
of death
of the Mother's breasts!

抓起工具随节拍挥动，肩并肩

闪动智能的光芒和沉默的知识

眼对眼

安坐像猫像蛇像石头

完整而包容一切

如黝蓝的天空。

温文天真如狼

狡黠如王子。

劳作而各就其位：

为了荒野

为了生命

为了死亡

为了母亲的乳房！

For the Children

The rising hills, the slopes,
of statistics
lie before us.
the steep climb
of everything, going up,
up, as we all
go down.

In the next century
or the one beyond that,
they say,
are valleys, pastures,
we can meet there in peace
if we make it.

To climb these coming crests
one word to you, to
you and your children:

给孩子们

隆起的山丘和斜坡，
这统计表的曲线
展开在我们面前。
一切都在
陡峭地攀高，
攀高，当我们全都
坠下。

下个世纪
或再下个世纪，
他们说，
如果我们做
就会有山谷、草原，
我们就可以在那儿和平地相遇。

要攀过这些迎面而来的山脊
给你一句话，给
你和你的孩子们：

stay together

learn the flowers

go light

Gary Snyder

团结一处

学习花朵

轻快前进

Axe Handles

One afternoon the last week in April
Showing Kai how to throw a hatchet
One-half turn and it sticks in a stump.
He recalls the hatchet-head
Without a handle, in the shop
And go gets it, and wants it for his own.
A broken-off axe handle behind the door
Is long enough for a hatchet,
We cut it to length and take it
With the hatchet head
And working hatchet, to the wood block.
There I begin to shape the old handle
With the hatchet, and the phrase
First learned from Ezra Pound
Rings in my ears!
"When making an axe handle
        the pattern is not far off."
And I say this to Kai
"Look: We'll shape the handle
By checking the handle

斧子把

四月最后一周的某个下午
教开（Kai）怎样抛掷战斧
它旋飞半圈剁进树桩。
他想起商店里，一个
没有柄的战斧头
便去找它，想据为己有。
门后有一根断掉的斧子把
长得足以做战斧柄，
我们把它锯成想要的长度，
把它与战斧头
还有工作斧一起拿到木墩上。
于是我开始用工作斧
劈砍那根旧斧子把，早先
从埃兹拉·庞德那儿学到的说法
鸣响在我耳畔！
“伐柯伐柯
　　其则不远。”
而我对开（Kai）这样说
“瞧：我们会根据
我们砍木头的斧子的把

Of the axe we cut with—"
And he sees. And I hear it again:
It's in Lu Ji's *Wên Fu,* fourth century
A.D. "Essay on Literature"—in the
Preface: "In making the handle
Of an axe
By cutting wood with an axe
The model is indeed near at hand."
My teacher Shih-hsiang Chen
Translated that and taught it years ago
And I see: Pound was an axe
Chen was an axe, I am an axe
And my son a handle, soon
To be shaping again, model
And tool, craft of culture,
How we go on.

砍出战斧柄的形状——”

他明白了。我再次听见：

公元四世纪陆机

在《文赋》序言中

说：“至于

操斧伐柯

虽取则不远。”

我的老师陈世骧[1]

多年前就译出并讲授它

而我明白了：庞德是斧子，

陈是斧子，我是斧子

而我的儿子是斧子把，很快

会被塑造一新，模型

和工具，文化的技艺，

我们就这样延续。

1 陈世骧（1912—1971），美籍华人学者。字石湘。生于河北。1932 年获北京大学文学士学位。曾任北京大学、湖南大学讲师。1941 年赴美留学，在哥伦比亚大学攻读西洋文学批评，并一度在哥大执教。1947 年起任教于伯克利加州大学中文系，历任助理教授、副教授、教授和东方语文学系主任，主讲中国古典文学及中西比较文学。盖瑞·施耐德曾在他的指导下学习中国古典诗歌。

Working on the '58 Willys Pickup

for Lu Yu

The year this truck was made
I sat in early morning darkness
Chanting sūtra in Kyoto,
And spent the days studying Chinese.
Chinese, Japanese, Sanskrit, French—
Joys of Dharma-scholarship
And the splendid old temples—
But learned nothing of trucks.

Now to bring sawdust
Rotten and rich
From a sawmill abandoned when I was just born
Lost in the young fir and cedar
At Bloody Run Creek
So that clay in the garden
Can be broken and tempered
And growing plants mulched to save water
And to also haul gravel

整修58年威利式皮卡

给陆游

这卡车造好那一年
我正在京都
坐在黎明的幽暗里诵经,
整天学习中文。
中文、日文、梵文、法文——
修习佛法的欢愉
还有那壮丽的古老寺庙——
但没学过修卡车。

我用它从布拉迪伦溪
那隐没在年轻的冷杉和雪松间的锯木厂
一家我出生时就已弃置的锯木厂
运回了木屑
又懈烂又肥沃
可用以掺入并调和
花园里的泥土
保护植物的根,不让水流失——
还可以挂住沙砾

From the old placer diggings,
To screen it and mix in the sand with the clay
Putting pebbles aside to strew on the paths
So muddy in winter—

I lie in the dusty and broken bush
Under the pickup
Already thought to be old—
Admiring its solidness, square lines,
Thinking a truck like this
would please Chairman Mao.

The rear end rebuilt and put back
With new spider gears,
Brake cylinders cleaned, the brake drums
New-turned and new brake shoes,
Taught how to do this
By friends who themselves spent
Youth with the Classics—

The garden gets better, I
Laugh in the evening
To pick up Chinese

好对付过去挖矿造成的土质松垮，
把它筛过再混合泥沙
铺好小路再缀上卵石
那么冬天来时便不再泥泞——

我躺在多尘的断枝的灌木间
躺在这辆皮卡下
已经算旧了——
但我欣赏它的结实，规矩的线条，
心想这样一辆货车
会让毛主席喜欢。

车尾重新造过并且换上了
新的细长的排挡，
刹车的机筒清理过，刹车轮
刚转过又加上新的刹车脚踏，
教我这么做的
朋友们年轻时
也曾遍读经典——

花园变得更好，我
笑在晚上
捡起中文书

And read about farming,

I fix truck and lock eyebrows

With tough-handed men of the past.

读一读农事,

我修理皮卡，然后凝眉于

从前那些干活的好手。

Dillingham, Alaska, The Willow Tree Bar

Drills chatter full of mud and compressed air
all across the globe,
        low-ceilinged bars, we hear the same new songs

All the new songs.
In the working bars of the world.
After you done drive Cat. After the truck
                went home.
                Caribou slip,
                front legs folded first
                under the warm oil pipeline
                set four feet off the ground—

On the wood floor, glass in hand,
                laugh and cuss with
                somebody else's wife
                Texans, Hawaiians, Eskimos,

阿拉斯加州迪林佳木，柳树酒吧

钻头哐哐塞满泥巴和压缩空气，
全球到处，
　　在低矮的酒吧里，我们听到同样的新歌

总是新歌。
在世界上的干活人的酒吧里。
在你停下重型机车之后[1]。在卡车
　　　　归家之后。
　　　　大北极鹿摔跤，
　　　　先屈前腿
　　　　在暖和的石油管道之下[2]
　　　　四蹄蹬开在地上——

木地板的酒吧，酒杯在手
　　　　笑骂
　　　　别人的老婆
　　　　得克萨斯人、夏威夷人、爱斯基摩人、

1　原文 Cat，当系 Caterpillar 公司的缩写。该公司主要生产大型履带式机械工程车，如推土机、挖土机等。

2　阿拉斯加石油管道的架设一般距地面有些距离。

Filipinos, Workers, always
on the edge of a brawl—
In the bars of the world.
Hearing those same new songs
in Abadan,
Naples, Galveston, Darwin, Fairbanks,
White or brown,
Drinking it down,
the pain
of the work
of wrecking the world.

菲律宾人，工人们，总是

一副说干架就会干起来的样子——

在世界上的酒吧里。

在阿巴丹、那不勒斯、高威斯顿、达尔文

费尔班克

听到那些同样的新歌

白人或棕褐色的人们，

喝下，

劳作

和打穿世界的

痛苦

Uluru Wild Fig Song

1

Soft earth turns straight up
curls out and away from its base
hard and red—a dome—five miles around
                    Ayers Rock, Uluru,

we push through grasses, vines, bushes
along the damp earth wash-off watershed margin
    where vertical rock dives
        into level sand,

Clustering chittering zebra finches on the

乌鲁汝野无花果之歌

1

柔软的泥土直立而起
从其底部开始弯转开来
硬而红色——一座教堂——周围五英里
　　　　　　艾尔斯巨岩，乌鲁汝[1]，

我们沿着被冲刷的分水岭边缘的湿地
穿过草丛、藤蔓和灌木
　　那里耸立的岩石
　　　　沉入沙地，

道道黑纹的斑胸草雀立在

1　乌鲁汝，系指艾尔斯岩，位于澳大利亚中北部的艾丽斯斯普林斯 (Alice Springs) 西南方向约 340 公里处。艾尔斯岩高 348 米，长 3000 米，基围周长约 9 公里，孤零零地奇迹般地凸起在荒凉无垠的平坦荒漠之中。其较低的斜坡上由于较弱岩层的蚀化而出现沟槽，而顶部有因罕见的暴雨所带来的大水冲刷出的沟渠和洼地。其底部有一些浅洞穴，被某些原住民部落视为圣地，洞内有雕刻和绘画。地貌周围生有蓝灰檀香木、红桉树、金合树等。土著人称这座石山为“乌鲁汝”，意思是“见面集会的地方”。西方人称之为“艾尔斯岩”，它的得名可追溯到 1873 年，一位名叫克里斯蒂· 高斯的欧洲地质测量员到此勘探，意外地发现了这一世界奇迹，由于他来自南澳洲，故以当时南澳洲总理亨利· 艾尔斯的名字命名这座石山。

bone-white twigs,

red-eyed pink-foot little dove,

push on, into caves of overhangs,

painted red circles in circles,

black splayed-out human bodies,

painted lizards, wavy lines.

skip across sandy peels of clean bent bedrock

stop for lunch and there's a native fig tree

heavy-clustered, many ripe:

someone must have sat here, shat here

long ago.

2

Sit in the dust

take the clothes off. feel it on the skin

lay down. roll around

run sand through your hair.

nap an hour

bird calls through dreams

now

白骨一般的枝条上，
红眼粉爪的小鸽子，

努力向前，进入岩石垂挂的山洞，
但见红色的圆圈套圆圈，
黑色的伸展开的人类的身体，
还有蜥蜴和波纹线。

跨过好干净的岩床那沙砾般的碎屑
停下吃午饭，那儿有一株无花果树
簇簇沉甸甸的无花果，许多已经成熟：
必曾有人在这里长坐，拉屎
多年以前

2

坐于尘土
脱衣。感觉尘土扑上皮肤
躺下。翻身
沙子穿过你的头发。
打盹一小时
梦中鸟鸣
现在

you're clean.

sitting on red sand ground with a dog.
breeze blowing, full moon,
women singing over there—
men clapping sticks and singing here

eating meaty bone,
hold the dog off with one foot

stickers & prickles in the sand—

clacking the boomerang beat,
a long walk
singing the land.

3

naked but decorated,
scarred.
white ash white clay,
scars on the chest.
lines of scars on the loin.

你清洁。

坐在红色的沙子上一狗相伴。
微风送爽，满月，
女人在那边歌唱——
男人在这边歌唱并用木棍敲打出节拍

啃带肉的骨头，
用一只脚带住狗

沙土中的牵衣的草根和刺儿——

打出飞去来器的啪啪节拍，
远足
歌唱大地。

3

赤裸但装饰着，
疤痕。
白色的灰烬　白色的泥，
疤痕在胸脯上。
腰间线纹的疤痕。

the scars: the gate,

the path, the seal,

the proof.

white-barred birds under the dark sky.

4

singing and drumming at the school
a blonde-haired black-skinned girl
watching and same time teasing a friend
dress half untied, naked beneath,
young breasts like the mulpu
mushroom,
swelling up through sand.

stiff wind close to the ground,
trash lodged in the spinifex, the fence,
the bottles, broken cars.

疤痕：　这大门，

这路径，这封印，

这证据。

白色疤痕的鸟在暗沉沉的天空下。

4

一个金发而肤色褐暗的姑娘

在学校唱歌并打鼓

张望，同时逗着一个朋友

那位扣子半解，衣服里身子裸赤，

年轻的乳房有如 mulpu [1]

蘑菇

膨胀着拱出沙子。

贴近大地风是硬的，

垃圾聚集于三齿稃，那栅栏，

有瓶子，报废的汽车。

1　澳大利亚边地土语，意指蘑菇。

5

Sit down in the sand

skin to the ground.

a thousand miles of open gritty land

white cockatoo on a salt pan

hard wild fig on the tongue.

this wild fig song.

Fall of 40081, Uluru, Amata, Fregon,

Papunya, Ilpili, Austral.

5

坐下在沙子中

　　皮肤贴地。

　　辽阔的千里沙砾之地

　　白色的美冠鹦鹉在一只盐铁盘上

硬硬的野无花果在舌头上。

　　这野无花果之歌。

40081 秋天，乌鲁汝，阿玛塔，弗莱根，

巴普尼亚，伊皮里，澳洲。

Old Woman Nature

Old Woman Nature
naturally has a bag of bones
    tucked away somewhere.
    a whole room full of bones!

A scattering of hair and cartilage
  bits in the woods.

A fox scat with hair and a tooth in it.
  a shellmound
    a bone flake in a streambank.

A purring cat, crunching
  the mouse head first,
  eating on down toward the tail—

The sweet old woman
  calmly gathering firewood in the
      moon ...

老妪自然

老妪自然
自然有一袋骨头
　　　　藏在某处。
　　　　整个房间里到处是骨头！

林中四处星星点点
　　抛撒着头发和软骨。

头发和缠在其中的一颗牙惊走了狐狸。
　　堆起的贝壳
　　　　溪岸上的骨头渣。

喉咙里咕噜有声的猫
　　先嚼碎老鼠的头，
　　　　然后一直吃到它的尾巴——

月亮上
　　甜甜的老妪安静地收着
　　　　柴火……

Don't be shocked,

She's heating you some soup.

VII 81, Seeing Ichikawa Ennosuke in

"Kurozuka"-"Demoness"-at the Kabuki-za in Tokyo

别吓着，

她在为你炖锅汤。

VII 81，在东京歌舞伎座的“黑冢”

演出中看到市川猿之助

Longitude 170° West, Latitude 35° North

for Ruth Sasaki

This realm half sky half water,
    night black with white foam
    streaks of glowing fish
    the high half black too lit with
    dots of stars,
The thrum of the diesel engine twirling
    sixty-four-foot drive shafts of twin screws,
Shape of a boat, and floating
    over a mile of living seawater, underway,
    always westward, dropping
    land behind us to the east,
Brought only these brown Booby birds that trail
    a taste of landfall feathers in the craw
    hatchrock barrens—old migrations—
    flicking from off the stern into thoughts,
Sailing jellyfish by day, phosphorescent
    light at night,
    shift of current on the ocean floor

西经170°，北纬35°

为鲁思·佐佐木而作

这片海域一半天空一半海水，
　　黑色的夜，白色的浪沫
　　奔游的鱼，闪光的行迹
　　高阔而黑暗的夜空
　　也是星光点点，
柴油发动机突突转动
　　双机传动轴长六十四英尺
船形，在一英里
　　颠簸的海水上漂浮，航行，
　　一直向西，将身后的
　　陆地朝东方甩远，
只有这些棕色的呆鸟追随
　　嗉子里遥盼着落地的羽毛
　　那不毛之地——古老的迁徙——
　　它们从船尾拍翅飘入思想，
白天航游的水母，到夜晚
　　发出磷光，
　　海底水流转换

food chains climbing to the whale.

Ship hanging on this membrane infinitely
tiny in the "heights" the "deep"
air-bound beings in the realm of wind
or water, holding hand to wing or fin
Swimming westward to the farther shore,
this is what I wanted? so much
water in the world and so much crossing,
oceans of truth and seas of doctrine
Salty real seas of our westering world,
Dharma-spray of lonely slick on deck
Sleepy, between two lands, always a-
floating world,
I go below.

M.S. Arita Maru, 1956

食物链攀向鲸鱼。

船只附着于这无尽的水面
忽上忽下尽显渺小
被空气紧裹的生命置身于风
或水的王国，抓住鸟翼或鱼鳍
向西游向更远的海岸，
这是我所需要的吗？世上有
太多的水太多的穿越，
真理的大洋主义的大海
而这咸涩的真实的大海是我们向西的世界，
甲板上佛法泼出的孤独的平面
困倦，在两座陆地之间，永远是一个
飘浮的世界，
我下潜。

M.S. 阿利塔·玛汝，1956

Bomb Test

The fish float belly-up, for real—
Uranium in the whites
                    of their eyes
They've been swimming
Deep down where it's black when a
Silvery snow of something queer
                    glinted in
From cirrus clouds to the seamounts,
Through all the food chains,
Shrimp to tuna, the currents,
Riding the waves.

Kyoto

核弹测试

漂浮之鱼肚子朝上——真的
铀染进
　　　　它们的眼白
它们本来遨游在
黑色的深海，突然
什么怪东西银色的雪
　　　　闪入
从卷云到海山
穿过所有的食物链，
从虾到吞拿鱼，海流，
骑着浪。

京都

Straits of Malacca 24 Oct 1957

Soft rain on the
gray ocean, a tern
still glides low over
whitecaps
after the ship is gone

*

Soft rain on
                gray sea
a tern
        glides brushing
                        waves
The ship's silent
                wake

*

Fog of rain on
                water

马拉加海峡，1957 年 10 月 24 日

灰色大洋上
温和的雨，一船驶过
燕鸥依旧低低地
滑行在
白色浪沫之上

*

灰色的大海
　　　　　　温和的雨
一只燕鸥
　　掠过
　　　　浪峰
船只安静的
　　　　尾浪

*

雨雾
　　　　在水上

Tern glides

Over waves,

the

wake

燕鸥滑过
浪峰，
这
尾浪

The North Coast

Those picnics covered with sand
No money made them more gay
We passed over hills in the night
And walked along beaches by day.

Sage in the rain, or the sand
Spattered by new-falling rain.
That ocean was too cold to swim
But we did it again and again

北海岸

野餐食物上盖着沙子
没钱让他们更欢心
我们夜晚越岭翻山
白天走在大海边。

雨中的圣人，或沙中的圣人
被新落的雨再次打湿。
大洋太冷，不便游泳
但我们游了一遍又一遍

We Make Our Vows Together with All Beings

Eating a sandwich
At work in the woods,

As a doe nibbles buckbrush in snow
Watching each other,
chewing together.

A Bomber from Beale
over the clouds,
Fills the sky with a roar.

She lifts head, listens,
Waits till the sound has gone by.

So do I.

我们与所有生物一起发誓

吃一份三明治
在树林中工作,

一头母鹿小口吃着雪中的小灌木
相互看两眼,
一起咀嚼。

一架从比莱飞来的轰炸机
在云层之上,
用咆哮充满天空。

它抬起头，聆听,
直等到声音消失。

我亦如此。

The Persimmons

In a cove reaching back between ridges
the persimmon groves:
leaves rust-red in October
ochre and bronze
scattering down from the
hard slender limbs of this
slow-growing hardwood
that takes so much nitrogen
and seven years to bear,
and plenty of water all summer
to be bearing so much and so well
as these groves are this autumn.
Gathered in yard-wide baskets
of loose open weave
with mounds of persimmons just picked
still piled on the ground.
On tricycle trucks
pedaled so easy and slow down the lanes,
"Deep tawnie cullour" of sunset
each orb some light left from summer

柿子

山峦夹着山坳
柿子林：
十月锈红的叶子
这缓慢生长的阔叶树
枝条硬瘦
散射出赭石和青铜
它需要大量氮肥
好七年结果，
还需整夏充足的雨水
才能结果如此之多如此之好
就如今秋的柿子林。
一个个粗简编就的
一米宽的大筐里
堆着刚刚摘下的柿子
堆在地上。
小路上
脚踏三轮车缓慢而怡然，
车斗里的柿子有落日的深深的橙红色
每个柿子都留存着一点夏日的光
闪耀于秋天褐色的土地，

glowing on brown fall ground,
the persimmons are flowing
on streams of more bike-trucks
til they riffle and back up
alongside a car road
and are spread on the gravel by sellers.
The kind with a crease round the middle,
Tamopan, sweet when soft,
ripening down from the top to the base.
Persimmons and farmers
a long busy line on the roadside,
in season, a bargain, a harvest
of years, the peace of
this autumn again, familiar,
when found by surprise at
the tombs of the dead Ming emperors.
Acres of persimmon orchards
surrounding the tumuli
of kings who saw to it they kept on consuming
even when empty and gone.
The persimmons outlive them,
but up on the hills

更多的小三轮
汇成柿子流
直到它们来到公路上
乱堆然后排队等待
被售卖者摊开在沙砾上。
这种柿子中部收腰，
叫“大磨盘”[1]，软时更甜，
先熟在树顶上。
路边繁忙的一长溜
柿子和农民。
这是一年中收获、讨价还价的
季节，又一秋
惯常的平和
这场景令人惊讶
在那些明代皇帝的陵寝边。
大片的柿子园环绕着
帝王的坟墓，他们存心坚持消费
即使人去市空。
柿子树比他们活得更久。
但是在山上
长城蜿蜒之处
在成吉思汗的年代

1 原文 Tamopan，是“大磨盘”的音译。

where the Great Wall wanders
the oaks had been cut for lumber or charcoal
by Genghis Khan's time.
People and persimmon orchards prevail.
I walked the Great Wall today,
and went deep in the dark of a tomb.
And then found a persimmon
ripe to the bottom
one of a group on a rough plaited tray
that might have been drawn by Mu Ch'i,
tapping its infant-soft skin
to be sure that it's ready,
the old man laughing,
he sees that I like my persimmons.
I trade him some coin
for this wealth of fall fruit
lined up on the roadside to sell to the tourists
who have come to see tombs,
and are offered as well
the people and trees that prevail

Beijing, People's Republic, 1984

橡树被砍伐做木材或劈柴。
人和柿子园留存下来。
我今天漫步于长城，
并深入了一座陵墓的黑暗。
然后在一个盛着几枚柿子的
粗简编篮儿里发现了一枚
熟透的柿子
也许曾经被牧溪画过[1]，
碰碰它婴儿嫩的皮儿
看它是否已准备好，
老人笑了，
知我喜欢我的柿子。
我掏出几枚硬币
买下这秋天的财富秋天的果实
它们在路边码开是要卖给
来参观陵墓的游人，
也会白送
人和树留存下来。

北京，人民共和国，*1984*

1　牧溪俗姓李，佛名法常，号牧溪，四川人，生卒年月不详。南宋画家，日本古籍《松斋梅谱》中评价牧溪的绘画“皆随笔点墨而成，意思简当，不费装缀”。中国《画继补遗·卷上》载：“僧法常，自号牧溪。善作龙虎、人物、芦雁、杂画，枯淡山野，诚非雅玩，仅可僧房道舍，以助清幽耳。”其画笔墨淋漓，颇具禅意。遗迹多流日本，甚至被评为“日本画道的大恩人”。

Word Basket Woman

Years after surviving
the Warsaw uprising,
she wrote the poems of ordinary people
building barricades while being shot at,
small poems were all
that could hold so much
close to death life
without making it false.

Robinson Jeffers, his tall cold view
quite true in a way, but why did he say it
as though he alone
stood above our delusions, he also
feared death, insignificance,
and was not quite up to the inhuman beauty
of parsnips or diapers, the deathless
nobility at the core of all ordinary things

词篓之妇

幸存于华沙起义
多年之后，
她写诗关于那些迎着子弹
修筑路障的普通人，
只有小小诗篇
可以无限贴近
那生与死
不作假。

罗宾逊·杰弗斯[1]，他那冰冷高蹈的观点
某种意义上并没错，但他何必
仿佛独自站在
我们的错觉之上，他也
怕死，怕无意义，
他也没有攀上那铺开
防风草或尿布的非人类之美
那永生的高贵在俗常事物的核心

1　罗宾逊·杰弗斯（1887—1962），20世纪美国诗人，认为人事无常，仅上帝除外，人生不过是感情罗网中一场狂暴而可鄙的斗争。

I dwell
in a house on the long west slope
of Sierra Nevada, two hundred mile
swell of granite,
bones of the Ancient Buddha,
miles back from the seacoast
on a line of fiery chakras
in the deep nerve web of the land,
Europe forgotten now, almost a dream—
but our writing
is sidewise and roman, and the language
a compote of old wars and tribes from some
place overseas. Here
at the rim of the world
where the panaka calls in the chá—the heart
words are Pomo, Miwok, Nisenan,
and the small poem word baskets
stretch to the heft of their burden.

我居住在
内华达山脉长长的
西坡，是两百英里
隆起的花岗岩，
古佛的骨骼，
距海岸数英里
处于火热的能量穴[1]经络之上
在大地神经之网的深处，
已经忘了欧洲，那几乎是个梦——
但我们的书写
老套而无关痛痒，而语言
是别处土地上什么部落与古老战争的
糖渍果盘。这里
在世界的边沿
Panaka 啄木鸟鸣叫在 chá 橡树间[2]——这是
颇摩人、米瓦克人、尼森南人的心灵之词。
而小小诗篇的词篓
加重了他们的负担。

1　原文 Chakras，该词来自梵文，起源于印度古老的瑜伽体系，翻译为“轮”或“碟”，指位于脊柱的中枢神经系统所发散的能量层。Chakra 是接受、同化和转化生命能量的中心。

2　原文 where the panaka calls in the chá。Panaka 和 chá 均系盖瑞·施耐德所居区域印第安人的词汇，分别指“啄木鸟”和“橡树”。

I came this far to tell
of the grave of my great—
grandmother Harriet Callicotte
by itself on a low ridge in Kansas.
The sandstone tumbled,
her name almost eaten away,
where I found it in rain drenched grass
on my knees, closed my eyes
and swooped under the earth
to that loam dark, holding her emptiness
and placed one cool kiss
on the arch of her white
pubic bone.

VI 85, Carneiro Kansas

XII 87, Kitkitdizze

我兜了这么远来讲述
我的曾祖母
哈丽特·卡里考特的墓地
它独处于堪萨斯低缓的山脊上。
沙岩墓碑已经倾倒，
她的名字几乎无法辨认，
在雨水湿草中我找到它
跪下，闭上眼睛
猛然扑入地下
那肥沃泥土的黑暗，抓住她的空寂
在她那白色的耻骨架上
印下冰凉的一吻

VI 85，堪萨斯卡内罗

XII 87，吉特吉蒂泽

Kisiabaton

Beat-up datsun idling in the road
shreds of fog
almost-vertical hillsides drop away
huge stumps fading into mist
soft warm rain

Snaggy, forked and spreading tops, a temperate
cloud-forest tree

Chamaecyparis formosiana—
    Taiwan hinoki,
        hung-kuai   red cypress

That the tribal people call   kisiabaton

奇希亚柏栋[1]

破旧的达特桑车空转在路上

残絮般的雾

陡峭山坡浑然消失

大树桩融入

温和的暖雨

枝丫错节撑开的树冠，一株温带雾林之树

福尔摩沙扁柏属——

台湾桧，

红桧　红扁柏

部落居民叫它　奇希亚柏栋

1　本诗描述的是台湾阿里山神木，该树树龄达到三千余年。本诗以原住民称呼红桧的语音为标题，诗中更列举了红桧的五个名称。1953 年，神木遭雷击，1956 年 6 月 7 日又遭雷击，树心油脂被焚毁，阿里山神木死亡。1962 年，管理者邀请专家爬上树顶，搭设平台并种植十余棵桧木树苗，对外宣称阿里山神木起死回生。1997 年 7 月 1 日，经不起连番豪雨冲刷，神木已成半倒状。1998 年 6 月 29 日，管理者决定放倒神木。倾倒的树身就此横置于原地，供人瞻仰。

this rare old tree

is what we came to see.

IX 90, Ali-shan, Taiwan

我们来看的

就是这株稀有的老树。

IX 90，阿里山，台湾

Ripples on the Surface

"Ripples on the surface of the water—
were silver salmon passing under—different
from the ripples caused by breezes"

A scudding plume on the wave—
a humpback whale is
breaking out in air up
gulping herring
　　　　—Nature not a book, but a *performance*, a
high old culture

Ever-fresh events
scraped out, rubbed out, and used, used, again—
the braided channels of the rivers
hidden under fields of grass—

The vast wild
　　　　　　　　the house, alone.
The little house in the wild,
　　　　　　　　the wild in the house.

水面波纹

“水面上起波纹——
这是银色的三文鱼在下面游过——不同于
微风漾起的波纹”

奔浪的卷羽——
一头驼背鲸
冲起在空中
一口吞下青鱼
　　——大自然不是一本书，而是一场表演，一种
高古文化

历久常新的事
被刮净，被擦亮，被再用，再用——
辫状河汊
隐蔽于草地之下——

旷野
　　　孤独的房屋。
旷野中小小的房屋，
　　　房屋中的狂野。

Both forgotten.

No nature

Both together, one big empty house.

两忘。

无性

两聚，一间巨大的空屋。

Stories in the Night

In Native California the winter was storytelling time

Yesterday I was working most of the day with a breakdown in the system.
Generator 1, Generator 2, old phased-out Generator 3,
the battery array, the big Trace inverter— solar panels —
they had all stopped—cold early morning in the dark —
back to the old days, kerosene lamp—candles—
woodstoves always work—
the back up generator #3 Honda, cycles wrong?
Tricking inverter relay that starts the bulk charge?

Big Green Onan—fueled by propane—wouldn't start—
(one time turned out there was a clogged air cleaner; oil-drops blow back up from deep inside.)

(I try to remember machinery can always be fixed—
but be ready to give up the plans that were made for the day—go back to the manual—call up friends who know more—make some tea—relax with your

夜晚故事

冬天曾是加州土著讲故事的时间

供暖系统瘫痪，昨天几乎整天我都在忙活。
一号电机、二号电机、老旧的逐渐淘汰的三号电机、
电池组、巨大的电荷轨迹逆变器——太阳能板——
统统罢工——黑暗中冰冷的早晨——
回到往昔，煤油灯——蜡烛——烧柴的炉子从不出错——
三号本田替补电机，运转错误？欺骗了逆电器给指令开始了容积充电？

昂南[1]绿色的大机器——以丙烷为燃料——拒绝工作——
（有回发现是一个空气清洁器受堵；油滴从内部深处喷上来。）

（我努力记住，机械总可以修好——但已决定放弃一天的安排——回到体力活——叫来更在行的朋友——煮

1 昂南，像本田一样都是电机生产厂家。

tools and your problems, start enjoying the day.)

First fifteen years we lived here, kerosene lamps. Heavy tile roof in the shade of a huge pre-contact black oak;

Cheri, Siegfried's long-time woman friend and partner, is due at any time with a 9-ton truck of 3/4 inch crushed rock. Wet dirt every winter eats up gravel, keeping a few hard roads for drenching winter rains and melting snows
takes planning.   You have to ditch them too.

In 1962 going all through Kyushu with Joanne, walked around Nagasaki. Busy streets and coffee shops, green leafy trees and gardens, a lively place. But at Mt. Aso, great caldera in the center of the island, crater fifteen miles across, saw sightseers from Nagasaki with the twisted shiny scarred burn-faces of survivors from those days. And then read Barefoot Gen.

What got to me about the Bomb was too much power.

茶——守着你的工具和麻烦放松，开始享受这一天。）

我们住这儿的头十五年，用的是煤油灯。高大原生的黑橡树树荫里是我们沉重的屋瓦；

切莉，西格弗莱德长期的女友和伴侣，总开一辆 9 吨卡车携 3/4 英寸厚碎石，会随时出现。每个冬天湿泥吞尽沙砾，特意留出几条梆硬的路渗下冬雨和融雪。当然你也得在路旁挖沟。

1962 年与琼妮一起穿越九州岛，逡巡于长崎一带。那儿有繁忙的街道和咖啡店、葱绿的树木和花园，有生气的地方。
但在岛屿中部阿苏山庞大的活火山口，直径十五英里的火山口，看到长崎来的观光客，他们是那些日子的幸存者，被烤灼过的脸上闪着扭曲的疤痕。之后，读《赤脚根》[1]。

有关核弹我意识到其能量过大。

1　本书是讲述原子弹爆炸幸存者故事的多卷漫画集，作者为中泽启治。

And then temptation there to be ... the first.
The first to be "The Empeor of the World."
Yet to be done: So change our course around, or there we head.

I could never be a Muslim, a Christian, or a Jew because the Ten Commandments fall short of moral rigor. The Bible's "Shalt not kill" leaves out the other realms of life,

How could that be? What sort of world did they think this is?
With no account for all the wriggling feelers and the little fins, the spines, the slimy necks, —eyes shiny in the night—paw prints in the snow.

And that other thing, can't have "no other god before me"—like,
profound anxiety of power and jealousy and envy,
what sort of god is that?
Worrying all the time?
Plenty of little gods are waiting to begin their practice and learn just who
they are.

然后是成为第一……的诱惑。

成为第一个“世界皇帝”。

好在未成：那我们就改变进程吧，或改变我们的方向。

我永远不会成为一个穆斯林、一个基督徒，或一个犹太人，因为“十诫”在道德上还不够严苛。《圣经》的“不得杀戮”遗漏了其他的生命王国，

那会怎样？他们以为这是何样的世界？

不予说明所有弯曲的触须和小鱼鳍、脊椎骨、黏糊糊的脖颈——闪烁在夜晚的眼睛——雪地上的爪痕。

还有那个，不能要“当我面，无他神”之类，

那种对权能的深深的焦虑和嫉妒和钦羡，这是什么神？

时刻忧心忡忡？

许多小神在等待开始一显身手并学会知道自己是谁。

In North India, Fourth Century AD, some Buddhist Tantrick Teacher Lady said,
"That God called Yahweh to the west, he's really something. But too bad,
he has this nutty thing that he's
Creator of the world."
A delusion that could really set you back.

But returning to energy. I'll fix the Onan, give up on #3 it's too far gone
and next time get a backup with a cast iron block and water cooling
and a warranty good for centuries—put in a bunch more panels for the sun—

The old time people here in warm earth lodges thirty feet across
burned pitchy pinewood slivers for their candles,
snow after snow for all those centuries before—
lodgefire light and pitchy slivers burning—

don't need much light   for stories in the night.

II..09 / i. 2012

在北印度，四世纪，一些佛教坦陀罗[1]女教师声言，
“西方称耶和华的那个神，的确不凡。但是太坏，
他竟大言自己是
世界的造物主。”
这错觉真能叫你崩溃。

但回到热能话题。我会修好昂南电机，放弃三号电机
它已奄奄一息

下次要买一个铸铁水冷的替补电机
好用上数世纪依然不坏——还应安装起更多的太阳能板——

这里，昔日，三十英尺外，住在地球小屋里的人们
烧漆黑的松枝照明，
从前所有世纪里的一场场雪——
炭火之光和燃烧的松枝——

夜晚说故事　无须太亮。

2012.1.9

1　坦陀罗 Tantra（派生出 Tantrick 一词），原系一部印度教经典，信奉这部经典的人称性力派，为印度教三大派之一。该派认为女神从男神所得性力是宇宙万有创造的根源。性力派思想后来影响到佛教密宗。

盖瑞·施耐德年表

西川 编译

1930 年	5 月 8 日出生于旧金山。两岁前与家人移居西雅图。
1942 年	父母离异，与母亲和妹妹迁居俄勒冈州波特兰。对北美印第安人文化，尤其是印第安人对大自然的态度产生兴趣。就读于林肯中学。喜爱登山。
1947 年	就读于波特兰瑞德学院。结识菲利普·瓦伦，并通过瓦伦了解到威廉·卡洛斯·威廉斯的诗歌。
1948 年	当过一夏天海员。
1949 年	第一次读到英国人阿瑟·威利翻译的中国古诗。
1950 年	赴印第安纳大学语言研究所修习一年。其间自习禅宗冥想。
1951 年	自瑞德学院毕业，获人类学和文学学士学位。夏天在优胜美地森林干活。

1952 年	秋天移居旧金山湾区。
1953 年	入加州大学伯克利分校东亚语文研究所，随陈世骧学习中国古典诗歌并翻译寒山诗。边学习边从事伐木、筑路、森林瞭望等工作。
	在湾区结识金斯堡、凯鲁亚克、弗林盖蒂、雷克斯洛斯（王红公）等。
1955 年	10 月 13 日在旧金山六画廊主办诗歌朗诵会，金斯堡裸体朗诵《嚎叫》，“垮掉派”由此名声大噪，其文学文化实践被称作“旧金山文艺复兴”。
	有数月时间与凯鲁亚克同住在加州米尔山谷的一处小屋。
	有时旁听美国亚洲研究院课程。长谷川三郎与阿兰·瓦茨在此任教。
1956 年	获美国第一禅宗学院奖修金东渡日本，在京都修习禅宗佛教和东方文化，一住十二年。其中有六个月的时间与艾伦·金斯堡、琼妮·基格在印度、尼泊尔旅行，参禅礼佛，走访胜迹。他本人还到过斯里兰卡、印度尼西亚，甚至随一艘油轮到过土耳其伊斯坦布尔。

1958 年 杰克·凯鲁亚克出版小说《达摩流浪者》。小说主人公以施耐德为原型。

1959 年 旧金山 Origin 出版社出版施耐德诗集《砌石》(*Riprap*)。

1960 年 纽约 Totem 出版社出版诗集《神话与文本》(*Myths & Texts*)。该书后由纽约新方向出版社于 1978 年重新出版。

1962 年 在斯里兰卡旅行时从一位澳大利亚作家口中听到日本诗人七尾榊的名字，一两年后施耐德在京都见到七尾榊，遂成至交。

1965 年 旧金山 Four Seasons 基金会出版《砌石与寒山诗》(*Riprap and Cold Mountain Poems*)。该书后由华盛顿 Shoemaker & Hoard 出版社于 2004 年重新出版。

旧金山 Four Seasons 基金会出版诗集《溪山无尽六章》(*Six Sections from Mountains and Rivers Without End*)。该书的修订版《溪山无尽六章加一章》(*Six Sections from Mountains and Rivers Without End, Plus One*) 于 1970 年出版。

1966 年 英国伦敦 Fulcrum 出版社出版《诗选》(*A Range of Poems*)，书中含施耐

德所译日本诗人宫泽贤治的诗。

1966年　Griffin 出版社出版诗集《三世界、三王国、六道路》(*Three Worlds, Three Realms, Six Roads*)。

1967年　与金斯堡一同主办旧金山金门公园 Great Human Be-In 活动，嬉皮士运动由此受到全美关注。

伦敦 Fulcrum 出版社出版诗集《僻野》(*The Back Country*)。该书 1968 年复由纽约新方向出版社出版。

1968年　获列文森奖。获古根海姆奖修金。

1969年　自日本返回美国，此后一直生活在内华达山脉北部的玉巴河畔。

新方向出版社出版散文著作《大地家族》(*Earth House Hold*)。

纽约 Phoenix Book Shop 出版诗集《蓝天》(*Blue Sky*)。

1970年　新方向出版社出版诗集《观浪》(*Regarding Wave*)。

1972年　纽约布劳克波特州立大学学院出版诗

集《皮尤特涧》(*Piute Creek*)。

1974 年　新方向出版社出版诗集《龟岛》(*Turtle Island*)，书名取自美洲印第安人称呼大地的古语。

1975 年　因《龟岛》获普利策诗歌奖。

加州大学图书馆出版诗集《家中一切》(*All in the Family*)。

1977 年　旧金山 City Lights 出版社出版《古风：随笔六篇》(*Old Ways: Six Essays*)。

1979 年　华盛顿州 Copper Canyon 出版社出版诗集《为盖亚歌唱》(*Songs for Gaia*)。

加州 Grey Fox 出版社出版《他在父亲的村庄猎鸟》(*He Who Hunted Birds in His Father's Village: The Dimensions of a Haida Myth*)，系施耐德在瑞德学院的学士论文。

1980 年　新方向出版社出版《真正的工作：访谈与谈话，1964—1979》(*The Real Work: Interviews and Talks, 1964—1979*)。

1983 年　旧金山北点出版社出版诗集《斧子把》(*Axe Handles*)。

Grey Fox 出版社出版自传《穿越印度之旅》(*Passage Through India*)。

1985 年　成为加州大学戴维斯分校教授。

1986 年　北点出版社出版《留在雨中：新诗 1947—1986》(*Left Out in the Rain: New Poems 1947—1986*)。该书 2005 年由 Shoemaker & Hoard 出版社重新出版。

旧金山 James Linden 出版社出版诗集《岩石与树木的命运》(*The Fates of Rocks & Trees*)。

1990 年　纽约 Farra, Straus 出版社出版文集《荒野实践》(*The Practice in the Field*)。该书 2004 年由 Shoemaker & Hoard 出版社重新出版。

1992 年　纽约 Pantheon 出版社出版《无性：新诗及诗选》(*No Nature: New and Selected Poems*)。该书获国家图书奖提名。

1993 年　华盛顿州 Brooding Heron 出版社出版诗集《北太平洋水与土》(*North Pacific Lands & Waters*)。

1995 年　华盛顿 Counterpoint 出版社出版散文选《空间地点：伦理、美学与分水岭》

(*A Place in Space: Ethics, Aesthetics, and Watersheds*)。

1996 年　Counterpoint 出版社出版诗集《溪山无尽》(*Mountains and Rivers Without End*)。

1997 年　长诗《溪山无尽》获波林根诗歌奖。

1999 年　Counterpoint 出版社出版《盖瑞・施耐德读本：散文、诗歌与翻译》(*The Gary Snyder Reader: Prose, Poetry, and Translations*)。

2001 年　自加州大学戴维斯分校退休。

2002 年　新方向出版社出版《留神：诗文选》(*Look Out: A Selection of Writings*)。

加州伯克利 Heyday 出版社出版文集《巍峨的加州内华达群山》(*The High Sierra of California*)。

2004 年　Shoemaker & Hoard 出版社出版诗集《峰顶上的危险》(*Danger on Peaks*)。

获日本正冈子规国际俳句大奖。

2007 年　Counterpoint 出版社出版文集《躺在火上》(*Back on the Fire*)。

2008年　Counterpoint出版社出版由比尔·摩根编辑的《艾伦·金斯堡与盖瑞·施耐德书信选》(*The Selected Letters of Allen Ginsberg and Gary Snyder*)。

2009年　Heyday出版社出版诗文集《泰墨帕斯山地漫步》(*Tamalpais Walking*)。

加州大学戴维斯分校向施耐德颁发教师最高荣誉金质奖章。